the Army, in hospitals, and in other institutions.

Dr. Coburn writes with conviction about the minister's sense of duty to God and man. For anyone who is deciding whether or not to become a minister, his book is a valuable and realistic guide.

About the author . . .

JOHN B. COBURN received the A.B. degree from Princeton University and the B.D. from Union Theological Seminary. He was ordained to the Episcopal ministry in 1943. From 1944 to 1946 he served as a chaplain in the U.S. Navy aboard the *USS Sheridan* and was in Tokyo Harbor on V-J Day. He was the chaplain at Amherst College, Dean of Trinity Cathedral in Newark, New Jersey, and is now Dean of the Episcopal Theological School in Cambridge, Massachusetts. In 1961 he met informally with Christian leaders from behind the iron curtain, and he has served on boards of the Protestant Episcopal Church concerned with higher education. Dr. Coburn has published many magazine articles and is the author of *Prayer and Personal Religion*.

JOHN B. COBURN

MINISTER

CAREER BOOK SERIES
Under the Editorship of Charles W. Cole

Professor by Fred B. Millet
Lawyer by Talbot Smith
Physician by Dana W. Atchley
Architect by Robert W. McLaughlin
Nurse by Edith Patton Lewis
Journalist by Herbert Brucker
Minister by John B. Coburn

John B. Coburn

MINISTER
Man - in - the - Middle

The Macmillan Company, New York
Collier-Macmillan Ltd., London

The author wishes to thank the following: *The Christian Century* for permission to reprint an excerpt from "The Minister's Dilemma" by Samuel Blizzard, originally published in the April 25, 1956 issue of the magazine, copyright 1956 by The Christian Century Foundation; Harper & Brothers for permission to reprint from *Advancement of Theological Education* by H. R. Niebuhr, D. D. Williams, and J. M. Gustafson, copyright 1957 by Harper & Brothers; The Reverend Clement W. Welsh for permission to reprint from his article in *Forward Day by Day;* and to the *Amherst Alumni News.*

First Printing

Printed in the United States of America

Designed by Joan Laws

The Macmillan Company, New York
Collier-Macmillan Canada, Ltd., Galt, Ontario
Divisions of The Crowell-Collier Publishing Company

Library of Congress catalog card number: 63-8662

Foreword

IN TALKING TO PARENTS OF COLLEGE UNDERGRADUATES IN
recent years, I have noticed that many of them are deeply concerned if their sons do not make a relatively early decision on
their future careers. "John is almost through junior year," they
say, "and he doesn't yet know what he is going to do after he
graduates." Similarly, a good many seniors have told me that
they are planning to do their military service right after college
so as to have two or three more years in which to decide on
their future vocations. Sometimes it is necessary to make a
choice fairly early. It is, for example, easier to prepare for
entrance to medical school if the appropriate premedical courses
are taken beginning with the second year in college. But in general it is better to put off a decision as long as practicable, so as
to make sure it is the right one. On the other hand, to postpone
it too long may be a waste of time. The years in military service
do not usually, or even often, turn out to be very helpful in
focusing a young man's thoughts on his future calling. Normally
it is a good thing if a young man or woman reaches a relatively
firm career choice during the last two years of college. But it is
also most advisable for a young person to start thinking about
the problem in secondary school, for it is never too early to
begin gathering facts, assessing interests and abilities, and trying
experiments, as with summer employment.

As a matter of fact the choice of a vocation or profession has
become a peculiarly complicated one for young men and young

women today. It involves an assessment of their own capabilities, an understanding of the modern world, and even a prediction as to the future. It normally involves, too, a good deal of soul-searching, fact-finding, and advice-seeking. That help for young people in making their career plans is increasingly needed I am utterly sure. Indeed, a choice of vocation has become much more difficult than it used to be. In part, the increasing difficulty arises from the obvious fact of the rapidly growing complexity of our society. There are literally hundreds of new callings, professions, and vocations, from airport traffic director and airline stewardess to hospital manager, business consultant, or television scriptwriter—all unheard of thirty or forty years ago. Some old callings have disappeared. At the turn of the century every village had a blacksmith. Now it is hard to find one. At the same time, many ancient professions have become more complicated, subdivided, and specialized. No longer does a young man merely decide to be a lawyer. He must also choose eventually among private practice, government service, and work for a single corporation, and also among the various legal specialties from admiralty law to taxes.

Partly it has become harder to choose among careers today because, for many of them, not only is a college education required but also some training after the four-year college course is necessary or desirable. Many engineers take one or two years of graduate work beyond the bachelor's degree before beginning to practice their profession. Increasingly, young men who are planning to enter business go for one or two years to a graduate school of business administration, or perhaps substitute for that, advanced work in accounting or economics. A high school teacher used normally to have just a B.A. or a B.S. degree. Now most of them have master's degrees, and some have gone on to take the doctorate. Today, many girls who are going into nursing take five or even six years in one combination or another of college and nursing school. To some degree, it is an indication

of how affluent our society has become that so many young
people can spend so many years in preparation for their life-
work. But even more the prolongation of education arises from
the needs and requirements of the most technically and socially
complicated society the world has ever seen.

Still another factor making for an increase in the difficulty of
vocational choice is the growing tendency to self-analysis among
students. Heirs to some decades of spreading information and
misinformation about psychiatry; victims of hundreds of mental
tests, projective tests, and aptitude tests; beneficiaries of a deep-
ening concern in school and home about problems of "adjustment"; it is no wonder if a young man hesitates long and pain-
fully before he reaches a conclusion about his own abilities,
motives, and goals.

Watching young men in college, I noticed a fact that seemed
odd to me, an observation that is really the genesis of this
Career Series. A good many students entering college think they
have already chosen a life vocation. Most of those who plan to
be physicians stick to that decision. But most of those who consider themselves pre-engineers abandon that idea during the next
four years. Even in the engineering schools that are most selective, the proportion of dropouts and failures among the undergraduates is surprisingly high.

Why should premedical students differ from pre-engineering
students in the firmness of their intentions and decisions? As I
pondered this question and talked to students in both categories,
the answer became utterly clear. The typical premedical student
has a fairly well defined notion of what a doctor really does. He
has been to a doctor's office. He has been to a hospital either
as a patient or as a visitor. He has read articles on the marvels
of modern surgery and the new wonder drugs. In a biology class
in secondary school he has already dissected a frog and a rat.
And the idea of healing people, even by complex techniques, is
basically a simple one.

The normal pre-engineering student, on the other hand, has only the vaguest understanding of what the work of an engineer is really like. Perhaps he thinks of it as mainly building bridges. He has no conception of the differences between chemical engineering, civil engineering, and aeronautical engineering. Nor does he realize that the most rigorous training in basic science and mathematics is part of the necessary equipment for an engineer. When, in college, he comes to a really difficult course like Differential Equations, he may suddenly discover that his aptitudes are more limited and his tastes less mathematical than he had thought. He reassesses his earlier decision and alters his career plan, but often with some lost motion and an impairment of his motivation.

Considering the problems in connection with career choices that all young men and women are facing, and realizing that what they need most to help them is truly authentic information about the various professions and vocations, it seemed evident to me that a series like this one would be most useful. Discussion with a number of educators and guidance counselors confirmed the idea, and The Macmillan Company welcomed it as an opportunity to be of real service to young people in secondary school and college.

The plan for the series as it has developed calls for a limited number of books on the most important vocations. Each is written by a person who has actually practiced and is intimately acquainted with the calling in question, and who has achieved notable distinction in it. Each is designed to present the problems of entrance into and practice of the different professions. But we hope the volumes will do more than that, for they are also intended to give a vivid picture of what it is like to be a lawyer, or a professor, or a minister. They attempt, moreover, to convey a sense of the personal requirements, the rewards and the sacrifices involved in the various vocations. There is no attempt to romanticize the professions. What these books are supposed to do is to help young people in the most practical possible way in one of the two most important decisions of life (the other being marriage).

In many ways *Minister* was the most difficult book to write in the whole series, for in addition to all the kinds of qualifications necessary for the other professions, the minister must have certain rather special personal qualities, some of them not easy to define or assess. Then too he must have a deep and sincere religious faith and the view of life and the purposiveness that spring from it. The Reverend John B. Coburn is peculiarly qualified to write this book, for two reasons.

First, he has had a rich and varied career in the various phases of religious work. After graduating from Princeton, he taught for three years at Robert College in Istanbul, Turkey, an institution founded with definite mission objectives. He returned to the United States, received his B.D. degree from Union Theological Seminary, and then served for two years as assistant minister in Grace Church, New York City. During that service he was ordained to the ministry in the Protestant Episcopal Church (1943). From 1944 to 1946 he was a chaplain in the United States Navy, and for the next seven years he was both rector of Grace Church in Amherst, Massachusetts, and at the same time chaplain of Amherst College. His next post was that of Dean of Trinity Cathedral, Newark, New Jersey, which he left to become Dean of the Episcopal Theological School, in Cambridge, Massachusetts. He is the author of *Prayer and Personal Religion* (1957). Thus Dean Coburn has served as a parish minister both in an urban and in a rural church, as a chaplain both in the Navy and in a college, and as an administrator in both a cathedral and a theological seminary.

The second reason arises from Dean Coburn's own qualities that he shows forth in this book. By the way he writes, the way he thinks, the way he feels, the way he looks at life, he makes the reader understand what a true minister must be like. The patent

depth and sincerity and persuasiveness of his Christian faith
come through on every page, but with simplicity and humility
rather than with didactic or doctrinaire preachments. He faces
the hard problems about the ministry, including even that of the
difficulties that may confront a minister's wife. All through the
book he tries to help a young man answer the question, "How
can I decide whether or not I ought to be a minister?" It is my
belief that reading this volume will be of tremendous assistance
to anyone who is asking himself that question.

The spirit of the book is nonsectarian. While it is written by
a Protestant and primarily for Protestants, Dean Coburn thinks,
and I agree, that it may prove useful, too, to young Roman
Catholics and to Jews who are thinking of going to a seminary.

CHARLES W. COLE

Santiago, Chile
1962

Introduction

THE PURPOSE OF THIS BOOK IS TO PRESENT THE CASE FOR THE ministry to men who are concerned about how their lives may count significantly in the latter half of the twentieth century.

It is written primarily for the college student who is in the process of coming to a decision about what he will do with his life. It is also intended to be of help to the college graduate who is already employed but who is not satisfied that what he is doing should be his life's work. Although it is written primarily with the Protestant ministry in mind, the basic considerations presented may be of help to the thinking of Roman Catholic and Jewish students as well.

This college student or graduate may be a Christian and a member in good standing of some church. He may, on the other hand, be quite uncertain about God's existence, have little faith in him, and hold membership in no church. Neither Christian conviction nor Christian behavior is a required condition for the reading of this book or for a preliminary consideration of the ministry.

What is required is honesty in looking at oneself, a desire to contribute to the human enterprise in general and to the lives of people in particular, and a serious intention to be identified with the best hope of mankind.

It may be that with such a beginning some will come finally to the conviction that for them that identification is best found in the ministry of the church—that is, in service to both men and God.

Some of the material incorporated in this book was presented in the Lowell Lectures, given in King's Chapel, Boston, in March, 1962.

For assistance in the preparation of the book I am indebted to two friends and former colleagues, Charles W. Cole, the editor of the Career Series, and Robert McAfee Brown, both of whom have read the first draft of the manuscript and have made many helpful suggestions.

Finally, I am eternally grateful to those to whom I have been sent to minister—my wife and children, congregations, students, teachers—and who have ministered unto me. It is they, some in this world and some in the next, who have taught me what the ministry is.

JOHN B. COBURN

Cambridge, Massachusetts
May 23, 1962

Contents

1

Men in the Middle
at Work

THE TELEPHONE RANG. THE MINISTER SWITCHED ON THE LIGHT
and looked at his watch. It was two-thirty in the morning. He
lifted the receiver.

"Hello, Mr. Jones speaking . . . Yes. Mrs. Gordon, what
can I do for you? . . . You have a question you want to ask
me? All right, what is it?"

Mrs. Gordon hesitated. She really had two questions. One was
to ask the clergyman a favor. This she knew he would do for
her. The other question no one could answer except God. But
God wasn't speaking to her these days—at least not so that
Mrs. Gordon could hear him. And this was the more important
question. Perhaps she could ask Mr. Jones—even if he couldn't
answer it.

"Mr. Jones. I just had a telephone call. It was the police.
Jamie's been in an accident. . . . No, he's not hurt. But he
ran over a man. . . .

"Yes, I guess he'd been drinking. But that's not all. Jamie
stole the car. It turned over and it's a total wreck. And the owner
is at the police station now and he's going to keep Jamie in
jail. They won't let me go see him. Tomorrow they said I could
see him. Tomorrow morning at ten o'clock. 'Bring a lawyer,'

they said. I asked, 'Can I bring my minister?' They said, 'Sure, bring your minister, but tell him to bring a lawyer.'

"So what I want to know first, Mr. Jones, could you go down with me tomorrow morning to the police station? And do you know some lawyer you could ask to come too? . . . You will? Thanks, Mr. Jones. Thanks ever so much . . . There is another thing now. There is another question I've got to ask you. Can you wait just a minute?"

She took a deep breath. The sharp pain came and went. Then it came again, more slowly, and seemed to linger inside her. Obviously she would have to go back into the hospital for another operation, the third in eighteen months.

She looked at the other side of the double bed. It was empty. For five years now it had been empty. Maybe life had been just too much for him. Too much had been expected. So he just took off. She didn't blame him really. He had had all he could take. And now she felt she had had about all she could take.

One husband and three children. And she had failed every one of them. Pete, the oldest, had been discharged from the County Reformatory after a three-month term and had enlisted in the Army. Now he was in Germany, and she almost never heard from him except for a card two or three times a year.

Elaine was the one she had put her hopes on. She was pretty, responsible, and bright. For four years in high school she had been on the honor roll and had been accepted at the state university. Then in the spring of her senior year she fell in love. He was a nice enough boy, but limited. His father was a chicken farmer and he was a chicken farmer. Elaine was suddenly possessed—there seemed no other word—possessed to marry him. So she did. They ran off and were married by a justice of the peace.

That was three years—three years and two babies ago, and

another on the way. Now they live in a tarpaper shack. When she comes to town she never says a word about anything except the children. Though she never mentions it, her mother guesses that what she is saying is: "I know it. I made it, I'll lie in it. Please, don't say it."

Now Jamie. Here he is sixteen. He had said he was off for an overnight hike with the Scout troop. He lied. It seemed he almost always lied.

She had never, she thought, been able to understand this boy. He had always been withdrawn and quiet. He had never caused much trouble. He just seemed surly. Now he had broken out and shown her how mad he really was. So he stole a car, and drank, and maybe killed a man.

One husband and three children, and she'd been no good for any of them. The pain began to ebb.

"I'm sorry, Mr. Jones, to keep you waiting like that. It's that other question. . . . It's this. What's the point in my going on?"

The officers came straggling into the wardroom. They had their life jackets on, and as they passed the door to the galley they picked up a sandwich and a cup of coffee. Then they put one arm around a stanchion, and, struggling to keep their balance, had one more meal—the eighth in a row—standing up.

Three days they had been in the typhoon, ever since leaving Naha on Okinawa. The ship kept heeling thirty-eight to forty degrees. There had been no sleep for anyone. You got thrown out of your sack every time the ship rolled. Chairs—and everything else that wasn't secured—were tossed about like matchsticks. Tempers were frayed, and as the officers drifted in—about twenty of them—no one had much to say.

Then the executive officer came in. He picked up his coffee and sandwich, took his place, and turned to the chaplain, who was on the other side of the wardroom. The only sounds were those of the wind howling and the ship creaking. Above the noise he bellowed:

"Hey, Chaplain."

"Yes, sir."

"I want to ask you a question."

"Very well, sir." Now what's coming? he wondered. It might be almost anything.

He had little love for the exec, and no respect. The wardroom bridge games on the way out from the Coast had netted the exec five thousand dollars. No one knew how he did it, but they all had their guesses. The chaplain had his guess too. It was the same as the others.

He wouldn't put anything past the man. On the first night out the exec had said to the officers, "Tomorrow morning General Quarters as usual one hour before sunrise. I want every man at his battle station—every man, that is, except the chaplain and me. Our battle stations are our sacks."

Maybe that was where the chaplain made his mistake, for he had spoken up: "Pardon me, sir, but my battle station is the sickbay. I'll be there."

"What are you going to be doing there, Padre? You'll do just as much good in the sack as you will in the sickbay or any-place else on this ship."

Well, that was the beginning, and it had set the tone of their relationship for the trip that followed. That was a year ago. So the chaplain braced himself, and thought, Here comes another one.

"Don't you want to know what the question is?"

"Yes, sir. I do."

"Why don't you ask me, then?"

"Very well, sir. What is the question you wished to ask me?"

"The question is: What the hell are you doing on this ship anyway?"

That's a good question, the chaplain thought. Not very original, though. In one form or another he'd been asked the same question ever since he joined the Navy. In fact it was a question he kept asking himself: What was he doing aboard that ship? What was a chaplain for?

On some ships the men knew what the chaplain did, even if they never responded to church call. There was an indefinable spirit that was on a ship if the chaplain was involved in the lives of the men. If he really cared for them, they knew it. And if he didn't care, they knew that too. That was when they kept asking, "What does the chaplain do, anyway?"

It all depended on the chaplain. There wasn't much of a built-in structure. In most of the churches back home the minister was somebody just because he was the minister. He had the support of the choir and the regular services and the church committees. Out here he was strictly on his own. He would sink or swim on how he did the job all by himself.

So he wondered at times how he did do his job. Two events stood out in his mind. The first had taken place in Zamboanga. They had been at sea for three months, and this was their first liberty port. The trouble with Zamboanga was that there was nothing for the men to do except go ashore and drink beer. So in his capacity as morale officer he went ashore to find some native entertainment.

He came back with a native band—bongo drums included. The floor show took place on Number 3 hatch. Men swarmed over the deck, and hung from the rigging; officers covered the bridge; there was not an empty place topside. It was the first live music anyone had heard since the Top of the Mark, and brought on a great jam session. The climax came when the twelve-year-old daughter of the bandleader appeared and gave an impromptu (and amateurish) hula dance. It wasn't the skill that counted. It was her spirit. The applause was thunderous. And never had the chaplain been so popular.

The other event was on V-J Day. The ship was in convoy approaching Tokyo Harbor. They were carrying seventeen hundred troops who that afternoon would be lowered into small boats and landed on the beach.

It was a Sunday morning, and he was conducting a Communion service topside. They were passing abeam of the *Missouri* while the peace treaty was being signed. Overhead rows of B-24's kept roaring in formation. They had come up from Okinawa, would pass over the fleet and harbor, turn, and pass over again.

He was distributing the bread; a chaplain with the troops was helping. Row after row of men came up. Wave after wave of bombers passed overhead. He wondered how the surrender ceremonies were going. Not that it made much difference. The war was over. No more broken bodies. No more broken minds. No more broken spirits.

No one knew what would happen to these young fellows. They'd be off in four hours. But they wouldn't be broken anymore. Down the rows, one after the other, placing the bread in their hands: "The Body of our Lord Jesus Christ, which was given for thee . . ." This is what's broken, boys. We're all kind of broken ourselves now. The whole world is broken. Maybe there will be healing now. But whether there is or not, this brokenness is what we have been given, and here is where all hope lies: ". . . preserve thy body and soul unto everlasting life."

That day, he thought, I *knew* what a chaplain is on this ship for. But now he'd better reply to the exec.

"That's a good question, sir, but I don't believe I'm in any position to answer it."

The wardroom was deathly silent. The wind and the creaking seemed only to deepen the silence. None of the officers said a word until the warrant officer spoke up.

"I think I can answer that question for you, Exec."

"Okay. You're such a smart fellow, what's the answer?"

The chaplain looked at the warrant officer, as did everyone else. He was a professional Navy man. He had been an enlisted man for fifteen years, and chief bosun's mate when the war broke out. Then he had been promoted. Socially he was out of his depth in the wardroom, but as a sailor and as a man he towered over everyone else.

Now, thought the chaplain, why should I feel closer to this man than to anyone else on this ship? He never attended any church service. He used loaded dice in the galley below when visiting troops were aboard. (For him—as for most in ship's company—the troops were the "enemy." "I'd never use loaded dice with ship's company," he had once confided to the chaplain.)

When men had liberty or leave and no money, he was the one they invariably went to to strike a loan. He would give anybody up to one hundred dollars, with no questions asked and no IOU's to be signed. He estimated that he had given away over five thousand dollars in three years, and all had come back except one thirty-dollar loan. "And that," he said, "was with a transfer who never did understand what this ship is about. People ought not to say," he philosophized, "sailors are no good. Sailors are good boys."

So here he was, a man who had no professed religious faith, whose morals stayed pretty close to nature, and who probably never had had a holy thought in his life. Why is it, the chaplain wondered, that I would trust this man with my life in a moment? Now, what do you suppose he's going to say?

"Come on," said the exec. "What's the chaplain doing on this ship?"

"Why," said the warrant officer, "the chaplain is here to pray for this ship and the men on it. That's why."

He had just received a phone call: "Please go across the square and meet the bus. Tell Johnny that his mother has just died. Bring him back to the house. His father will be there."

Eleven years old was young to lose a mother, he thought to himself as he walked across the square. He knew the family and he knew Johnny. He was glad he had been asked to break the news. There was the bus. Johnny got down. A quick flash of recognition and a delighted smile on his face when Johnny heard he was going to ride home the rest of the way in the minister's car.

Twenty minutes later, as the car turned into the driveway, Johnny turned to his minister: "I understand everything you said. I know that God is good. I know that he wants my mother to live with him, but what I don't understand is, 'Why did he kill her?' "

The minister and the sixteen-year-old girl climbed to the top of the hill. When they had sat down on the grass, they looked out over the valley. Below, the river wound its way through the fields; beyond, in the distance, the hills stood out in bold relief before the setting sun; colors began to rise and settle over the horizon.

"You know," the girl began, "sometimes when I come up here all by myself and look out over the river valley, I have an almost awful sense that God is here. It seems as though his spirit is brooding over the mountains and valley and that he is trying to say something to me. Can he really be here like that, do you think?

"Sometimes when I'm here I throw myself down on the grass and bury my face in it and smell the earth. When I look up, if it's twilight it sometimes seems as though the earth were standing still. Tell me, does this make any sense, or do you think I'm crazy?

"There have been two or three times when it's been even

worse than that. I don't mean 'worse' in a bad sense. It's been more terrible or awe-inspiring, even kind of scary. It seemed to me as I looked out that what I saw wasn't really real. It was as though some other world or spirit were breaking through into this world and that the only purpose of this world was to point to that other world. Everything seemed to merge together somehow: the river and the valley and those mountains and the sunset and even I. We all were part of one another and part of something greater, more beautiful, more holy than ourselves.

"I kept thinking that I ought to bow down and worship it. But I never did. When I walked down the hill, it was as though a door into another world had opened for me and another spirit belonging to that world had brushed against me, and I knew I'd never be quite the same again.

"Now, you're a minister. Tell me. Is that other spirit real, or am I just kidding myself?"

The minister was silent for several moments as he looked out over the valley and remembered what it was to be sixteen. He replied.

"No, you're not kidding yourself. That spirit is real. . . . It's as real as you are . . . as real as God is."

Everyone in the village knew Mrs. White. She hadn't been out of her house for twenty-five years. It was a little village, not more than a few hundred people. They all knew about how she had fallen and broken her back twenty-five years ago. Many of the old-timers still contributed five dollars a week as they had promised on that afternoon when the accident had taken place. They still came in every week or so to see her, and some of the young ones would stop by and say, "Hi, glad to see you."

One of those who came by every other week was the minister from the neighboring town. He would sit and read to her passages from the Bible:

"The Lord is my shepherd; I shall not want. He maketh me to lie down in green pastures: he leadeth me beside the still waters. He restoreth my soul . . ."

"Let not your heart be troubled: ye believe in God, believe also in me. In my Father's house are many mansions: if it were not so, I would have told you. I go to prepare a place for you. And if I go and prepare a place for you, I will come again, and receive you unto myself; that where I am, there ye may be also."

"Who shall separate us from the love of Christ? shall tribulation, or distress, or persecution, or famine, or nakedness, or peril, or sword? . . . . Nay, in all these things we are more than conquerors through him that loved us. For I am persuaded, that neither death, nor life, nor angels, nor principalities, nor powers, nor things present, nor things to come, nor height, nor depth, nor any other creature, shall be able to separate us from the love of God, which is in Christ Jesus our Lord."

One day after the minister had finished reading he offered a prayer to God. He thanked God for the courage he had given Mrs. White to bear faithfully her suffering; he remembered her husband who had died five years before, her three children, now married, the grandchildren and all those bound to her by ties of family and love "in this world and the next."

When he had said "Amen" and gathered up his coat to go, she said: "Can you wait a minute? I have a question I want to ask you."

"Certainly I can wait," he replied. "What is it?"

"What am I going to see when I die?"

He paused for a moment, his coat still over his arm. He thought of her patient spirit these past twenty-five years, of the loss of her husband, of the scattering of her family, and of the grace and strength that always came to him after his visits.

He replied, "You are going to see the face of God." He struggled into his overcoat and went out.

The discussion was going on in the fraternity house. It was part of "Religious Emphasis Week." The young visiting clergyman had just finished the presentation of his "case for Christianity." The fraternity brothers had listened politely. He waited now for the questions. They were not long in coming.

The first one: "You've been talking about God. How do we know there's a God? You can't prove there's a God. You admitted that yourself. If we don't know there's a God, how can we talk about him?

"What you say about faith being the way to the knowledge of God may be true enough. The fact of the matter, though, is I don't have that faith. Therefore for me God does not exist. There is no point in my getting mixed up with this God business until he or somebody gives me some faith. Isn't that right?"

The second one: "For the life of me, I don't see how you can make out any case for the church. Look at the people who go there: old women, little children, and a lot of defeated people. You don't find the leaders of the community there—not those with any vigor and vitality and drive. If they do go, it's just for the show and appearance of things. When they do go, they're bored.

"Besides, I don't see that going to church makes any difference in any way. Jewish boys around this college are just as good morally as Christian boys—some of them are better. Some of those church boys have the darnedest air of self-righteousness about them—but that's all they do have.

"I go to church every time I go home. I go to keep my mother happy. The minister is in a dream world, and talks about stuff that is utterly irrelevant. He's a nice enough fellow, but he has no brains. He once said, 'You have to close your mind, and believe.' No wonder the church is dead."

The third one: "I think you may have a point on that sex business. You're right that we ought not to use anybody just for our own selfish gratification. We ought to treat all women as human beings—even when they are willing not to be treated that way so long as you pay them.

"But I pinned my girl three years ago. I'm graduating this June. I've got two more years in business school. Our parents don't have any more money to put into education. We can't afford to get married, yet we love each other. We are genuinely concerned about each other. We are not trying to use each other. We simply want to express our love for each other the way God made us. When we trust each other like this, how can you tell us we ought to wait?"

The fourth one: "I just don't get this pitch about Christians saying they have the only understanding of God. What right have we got to go into other countries and tell perfectly decent people to stop worshiping God their way and come worship him in our way? How do we know Christ is so important? If I were brought up in a Buddhist country, why shouldn't I be a Buddhist? Why should Christian people tell me that it's better to be a Christian than a Buddhist?"

The minister began: "All right. Those are basic questions. Let's begin with the one on faith. Now, this is the way it seems to me. . . ."

The bus stopped at the railroad station. Twenty weary men and women, colored and white, climbed down and made their way into the station. The sheriff and two of his deputies who had been waiting followed them. He gave a speech they had heard several times now, ending with the familiar words ". . . and that means breach of the peace. You'll be arrested if you do."

One of the white clergymen made his way into the restroom marked *Men—Colored*. The sheriff and one of his deputies followed him. The sheriff said, "Hey, mister, are you one of them clergymen?"

"Yes, I am."

"If you're a minister, then what do you do things like this for?"

"Just because it's wrong. Do you want to know why it's wrong?"

It was Easter morning. The congregation was singing the last stanza of the sermon hymn "Jesus Christ Is Risen Today." The Reverend Mr. Brown has chosen that hymn because his text was "Christ Is Risen."

He mounted the pulpit steps and looked out over the congregation. There was standing room only. This was the third such service today.

There were not a great number of his own people that he could recognize. These were the twice-a-year Christians—Christmas and Easter. It used to upset him. When he was in the seminary he used to say to himself: "I'll tell those people. I'll tell them off so they will be really ashamed of themselves." And now he thought: What was the point of that sophomoric judgment? Here were people—come to hear the Word.

They could hear the Word now—if he could only preach it to them. Could he preach the Word? That was the question. Sure they came with the wrong understanding of the Resurrection. They thought of it as being like the lilies of the field that pop up every spring. God reigns because of Christ, not because of the bulbs in the ground and the tulips nodding their heads every springtime.

A strange thing, wasn't it? They didn't understand the Gospel, and yet here they were. Year after year they came. What was the mystery that brought them? How could they be captured for Christ? What was the one word for that season to strike fire in their hearts so that they might forever come to know the majesty of the Lord God Almighty?

They were here, and he was here. In some mysterious fashion God had brought them to these pews just as he had brought him in some mysterious fashion to that pulpit. Well, now, how was he going to introduce these people to God.

The hymn ended; the lights lowered; he began his prayer, "In the Name of the Father, and of the Son, and of the Holy Ghost. Amen."

The missionary sat in the classroom waiting for the boys to assemble. He had before him their examination papers. There were two sets. One set had been the first test in biology given six weeks after the semester began. The marks ranged from a low of 85 to a high of 100. He was suspicious, so he gave the same questions in a test the following week. There was that second pile with a low of zero and a high of 95. Forty percent of the class were under 50.

So here was knowledge of biology and here was honesty. He had come out as a missionary, commissioned by Christ to go into all the nations teaching, to lead them into all truth.

How, through the teaching of biology, was he to teach the truth of honesty? And how was the truth of honesty to be related to the truth of the Lord Jesus Christ? "I am the truth." How did he present that? What did he say now?

The bell rang. In came the boys. They sat down and looked up at him expectantly.

"Well, what did you learn in Sunday school this morning, Jimmy?" The question was asked by his father at the Sunday dinner table. Since his father had had a free morning except for taking Jimmy to Sunday school and picking him up afterward, he had completed the paper and was now going to give Jimmy his undivided attention.

"Well, I learned that Jesus loves me. That's what I learned."

"That's very interesting. Did you learn that Jesus loves you because the Bible tells you so?"

"No, not because the Bible tells me so, but because Mr. Martin tells me so."

"So then you know Jesus loves you because Mr. Martin says so."

"No, not because Mr. Martin says so, but because Mr. Martin does love me. That's why I know Jesus loves me."

"Who giveth this woman to be married to this man?" The father of the bride stepped forward and placed her hand in his. He took it, and placed it in the hand of the groom.

Look at those two hands joined together now, he thought. It's going to be important how they deal with each other, whether those hands stay open to each other or whether they become clenched. Well, his hand was here to help them remember that God's hand was in it; that God bound them together, indeed had brought them together, would always be with them together.

As they joined their hands and he withdrew his, he thought how often hands are used in the ministry.

I lift a little baby into my arms and dip my hand in the water and say, "John, I baptize thee in the Name of the Father, and of the Son, and of the Holy Ghost. Amen." Then I make the sign of the Cross on the forehead of the child, and say, "We receive this child into the congregation of Christ's flock." Later on, hands are laid on the heads of the children by the bishop in some churches or they are given the right hand of fellowship when they become members of their church.

And in time I get to recognize hands. They come and receive Communion, month after month, or week after week. I recognize the shapes. I don't have to see the faces after a while because I know the wrinkles in their hands. Some are gnarled and twisted; others are white, pale, and smooth. Some are rough hands; some are soft. Their faces are reflected in those hands; and year in and year out I place the Body and the Blood of Christ in them.

I raise my hand and tell them in public worship or sometimes in private, "Thy sins are forgiven. I absolve thee in the

Name of the Father, and of the Son, and of the Holy Ghost."
I want to shout it sometimes, that sign made by my hands: "You
are forgiven. Don't you get it? God forgives you. He wipes
away your sins. They're all gone. You are clean."

Then some days these hands take dirt and throw it in the
grave, "ashes to ashes, dust to dust . . ." Finally these hands
are raised to commend that soul departed into the everlasting
hands of God.

Well, here we are, near the altar now. "John, take Mary by
the right hand and repeat after me, 'I John take thee Mary to
my wedded wife . . .' Mary and John, join your two right
hands together. 'Those whom God hath joined together let no
man put asunder.' . . . Now you will kneel, please. Here is
my hand in a blessing. 'God the Father, God the Son, God the
Holy Ghost, bless, preserve, and keep you; the Lord mercifully
with his favour look upon you, and fill you with all spiritual
benediction and grace; that ye may so live together in this life,
that in the world to come ye may have life everlasting. Amen.' "

There you have it. Human hands touching. God touching
hands; men turning to God; God turning to man, offering himself into their human lives. God placing himself into human
hands . . .

How could you answer a question like that, anyway? His
college roommate had dropped in and asked him, "What are
you doing here?" He looked around the dingy room. It had
been a store and now it was a church. Though it was the middle of the afternoon, it was dark. It was dirty.

It was dirty and it was noisy. In the courtyard outside, boys
were shooting baskets. He could hear the thud of the ball against
the wall. Every time it hit, more dust came down. More kids
were out front on the street playing stickball.

Mothers came in, always wanting something: help to get on
relief, to get relief extended, old-age assistance, loans to tide

them over. Floaters came in sometimes. They floated up from the real lower depths downtown; they were the alcoholics, the bums. One look at their eyes and you could tell. You didn't even have to smell, although sometimes you couldn't help it.

What was he doing here? He never gave his roommate an answer to that. He wasn't certain himself, not absolutely certain—not so certain he could answer a friend's question. He certainly wasn't doing much good, he knew that. What he was doing anybody else could do. The church was no great success. A few came on Sunday. The best thing was the work with the kids.

That and working with the three other ministers who were with him. They didn't know either. They tried often to figure it out. As a matter of fact this was the question they kept asking themselves: What were they doing there? No results to date worth mentioning, but there they were.

Maybe that was the answer. They were there because they were there. The only important thing was that that's where they were.

It was like the story the Puerto Rican husband told him. He had taken a trip back to Puerto Rico. During his absence their baby had died. When he returned, his wife said to him, "The Reverend, he was here that night."

Her husband said, "What did he say?"

She said: "I don't know. He didn't say anything, I guess. But he was here."

It was kind of the husband to give him that report. He was touched. Well, that's the answer to his question. He was here—with the people. But how could you give your college roommate an answer like that?

These are all illustrations of men-in-the-middle at work. They describe some of the things that ministers do, the situations they find themselves in, the kinds of questions that are asked of them. This is by no means an exhaustive listing, but it may serve to point out certain constant features that are essential parts of the ministry. They are three in number.

The first is this: the ministry is always concerned with *people*. When you tell the story of a minister, you tell the story of people he touches.

"To minister" means literally "to serve." Ministers are called to serve people, to care for them, to be involved with them, to love them, to help them on their way. A minister is a man who is engaged with people.

The second factor is this: the ministry is always concerned with *God*. The minister is not only to serve people; he is also to serve God. Indeed, he usually will be trying to serve people because he wants to serve God. That service primarily is to help people in their relationship to God.

This relationship may be obvious, as when he conducts a service in church where people have gathered to worship God. The minister also stands at other "places of meeting" that are not so obvious. He deals, for example, with many people who do not believe in God. When he is able to help them affirm meaning for their lives, he is representing God even though he may never use religious words.

To say that a minister is concerned about people and God and the relationship between them does not mean he is concerned only with religious people, or good people. It means that he is concerned with all kinds of people, just because they are people. He is not necessarily trying to improve them, or to judge them, or even to make them religious. He wants simply to be with them where they are in their lives, whatever those lives be like. He wants to be able to serve them because they are members of a great, mysterious human enterprise.

There is, then, a third element in the ministry, and it is this: *mystery*. There is much about the lives of people that he does not understand; and there is even more about the ways of God that he cannot comprehend. He therefore affirms a great mystery about life. He does not try to minimize mystery, nor does he try to explain it away. Indeed, the longer he is in the ministry and the more he understands about God, the greater the mystery of life appears. So he does not come up with any cheap, easy answers about what God is doing. It is not enough to pat people on the back when they are down and say: "There, there, that's all right. God loves you."

The fact of the matter, of course, is that God does love them. Indeed, at the very heart of the mystery is this constant love of God for people. His job as minister is to show his people this love by his life as well as by his lips, so that they may know it too.

Sometimes all he is clear about is that God is as involved in the lives of his people as they are and that if they will only hang on to God, then God will pull them through. Within the mystery one thing is absolutely clear: "All things work together for good to them that love God." He knows this is true not simply because it is written in the Bible but also because it is written in life and he has experienced it himself. The individual purpose of each person's life is in some mysterious fashion bound up with God's ultimate purpose in the world. No matter, therefore, how tragic many experiences may be, life is good and worth living.

His assignment, then, put as simply as possible, is to help God and people meet. In the meeting people will come to know God. If they know who God is, then they will come to know who they are, and thus live as they are meant to live.

The minister is in touch with the power of God on the one hand, and with the lives of people on the other. Since he is "in-the-middle" he gets pulled and tugged. But if he is there because this is where God wants him to be, and where he wants to be, then he can understand all the pulling and tugging. Indeed, he can enter upon his ministry with joy and enthusiasm because it becomes his life.

This book, then, is about this kind of ministry. Its purpose is to help you who are reading it to come to some decision about whether you should go into this ministry.

You can begin to deal seriously with the decision by taking these as fundamentals in the ministry: people—God—mystery. If you are concerned about people (this doesn't mean you have to "like" everyone you meet); if you are concerned about God (this doesn't mean you have to know everything about him); and if you would like to be involved in the mystery of helping God and men meet; then you probably should go on to consider more closely what is involved.

To put it negatively: if you don't really care about people at all, if you are uninterested in God, and if you believe that there is no mystery in life that cannot be solved, then you might as well close the book now and put the ministry out of your mind forever.

If, however, you can honestly declare in some manner your interest in men and God and the mystery that surrounds us all, then you can in good conscience read on. What you read may at least be of interest to you, and at best may start you along a path that will lead you to a fuller understanding of this mystery and—who knows?—may place you one day "in-the-middle."

2

The Purpose of the Ministry

THE PURPOSE OF THE MINISTRY IS RECONCILIATION. MINISTERS are reconcilers. They are "in-the-middle" because men have become separated from one another and from God, and the minister's task is to bring them together again.

To put it another way, the purpose of the ministry is to help men realize that the complete meaning for their lives can be found only in relationship to God. This relationship is one that has already been established by God. It is that of a father to a son. It is expressed in the love that God has for each man, "as though he were the only one in the world he could love," [1] and the answering love of men to God as sons and to one another as brothers.

The ministry exists, therefore, that all men everywhere may understand this as the fundamental fact of their existence: they have been created by God so that they may come to know, love, and serve him and one another; they are related to one another as brothers and to God as their father.

Now, there may be little evidence that this is a true description. Most of the facts, indeed, point directly to the contrary

---

[1] "O Thou Good Omnipotent, who so carest for every one of us as if Thou caredst for him only, and so for all as if they were but one!" St. Augustine, *Confessions,* Book III, Chap. XI, 19.

conclusion: men do not act as brothers, and there is no proof that God, if indeed he exists, is at all interested in them.

Rather than relationship and reconciliation, separation and division seem to be more accurate descriptions of the human condition. Whether one looks at men in groups or individually (especially if one looks honestly at oneself), it is obvious that man is out for himself. The "survival of the fittest" seems a better key to unlock the mystery of what it is to be human than the "law of love."

The Christian does not deny these facts. Indeed, he claims it is essential to recognize them because they are facts of life. He would go even further and bring to light every evidence of suffering and sin and evil, examine every witness to the power of separation and division and self-seeking, make certain that the record reveals the worst.

He maintains that, although facts such as these have to be taken into account, there are also other facts that are part of the human picture. He takes the worst that man can present in order to go on and say that *even so* all men are brothers and God is their father. The sooner men realize this, he states, the better life will be for the human race, for then there will be a greater possibility for brotherhood and justice to prevail. He does not maintain that only Christians are the children of God nor that Christians are better than other men.

What he does claim, however, is that Christians have been let in on the secret of the mystery of life and can see (imperfectly, to be sure) how God is dealing with men. He is eager to accept all the facts of life that truly describe man, but then he takes a further step and says that the final description must always include the continuing action of God in the world. God, he maintains, has done and continues to do mighty acts. Those who have eyes of faith will be able to discern those acts, and in doing so will come to a more complete understanding of themselves and of all men.

The Christian looks at the same world and the same facts as the non-Christian. He sees the same divisions and suffering and selfishness. He sees them, however, from a different perspective. They are all seen as part of God's world, and not as ends in themselves. To help people view life from this perspective and to come to this understanding of their relationship to God so that they might be given strength by him is the business of the ministry.

It is the business of the ministry and it is the business of the church. More accurately, the purpose of the ministry is to enable the church to carry out its purpose: to let all men know who they are in relationship to each other and to God, and to live accordingly. This is the mission of the church, and it is carried out by lay people and ministers alike.

The Mission of the Church

This mission is sometimes referred to as the proclamation of the Good News. This is the Gospel that God was in Christ reconciling the world unto himself. Therefore—Christians maintain—people who have faith in Christ have nothing to be afraid of in this world: their sins are forgiven, and they can live a reconciling life of love themselves.

How this came to be is told in the Bible, where there is described what God did in the history of the Jewish people, in the life of his Son, Jesus Christ, and in his binding together by his Spirit those who believed in his Son. The Bible describes the actions of God, culminating in the great act of reconciliation in Jesus Christ.

God continues to act, Christians believe, throughout all the history that has followed and in the lives of his faithful people to this day. To proclaim—by their lives as by their words—

this continual reconciling act of God's love is the task of Christian people. This mission, indeed, is what the church *is*.

The resurrection of Jesus Christ from the dead is the evidence God gave that he is more powerful than either sin or death. He has, in fact, "destroyed" them. This means that he had overcome everything that separates man from himself and from each other.

This victory of Christ shows that the mind and will of God are love and that it is the most enduring force in the universe. No matter how much evidence there may be to the contrary, the final fact of life is that God can take the worst and turn it into the best. This is what he did when he sent his Son into the world and when he had died on the Cross raised him from the dead. It is what he has continued to do through the ages because this is his nature. This is the nature of love—never to be defeated, always reconciling.

After Christ left the human scene, those who had been his disciples and others who believed in him were bound together in an intimate fellowship by his Spirit. They prayed together in his name; they continued in the belief that Christ was the Lord over all powers set against him; and in accordance with his instructions they broke bread together as a memorial of him.

This was the beginning of the church. That is a word from the Greek *ecclesia,* meaning, "called out," "the congregation." For Jews, the word meant the people of Israel; and for Christians, those who confess Christ as Lord, who are the people of God.

The mission of the church was the same mission that had earlier been entrusted to the Jews: to make known to mankind the true nature of God as father of all men, who are therefore brothers. The Christians understood themselves to be commissioned to bring this Good News, together with the power to live as the children of God, to the far corners of the earth. They believed that God had created the church exactly for this purpose.

The original leaders of the church were the apostles. Under their leadership the church expanded so that local congregations were established in Jerusalem, Alexandria, Antioch, Rome, and other cities of the Near East.

The organizational structure of these congregations was adopted from Jewish congregational order. There was a council of elders. (This is a Greek word, *presbuteroi* translated "presbyter" or "priest.") This was presided over by a chairman or president or overseer. (The Greek word is *episcopos,* or bishop.) From the congregation members were selected to assist the bishop, originally in matters of business and relief, and later in the worship of the church, particularly in celebrating the Eucharist, as "the breaking of bread" came to be called. These were called deacons.

While the apostles were alive they transmitted their authority by laying their hands on and commissioning those chosen to be ministers with a prayer for the Holy Spirit. After the death of the apostles the ministers continued to be bishops, presbyters, and deacons. Later this authority was transmitted in a variety of ways—by the bishops themselves, by the council of elders, or on occasion by the congregation itself. By the middle of the second century the bishops had come to be accepted as the bearers of the apostolic authority who had the power to transmit it, and as the principal representatives of the church. From the time of the Reformation various traditions—Episcopal, Congregational, Presbyterian, and others—have emphasized different aspects of this authority within the churches.[2]

[2] Readers who are particularly interested in the question of how different denominations view the ministry are referred to a helpful pamphlet, "What the Churches Teach About the Ministry" (from *Laity,* No. 9, July, 1960, pp. 36–44), issued by the World Council of Churches, 475 Riverside Drive, New York 27, N.Y.

For our purposes it is enough to remind ourselves that, whatever the tradition, there is one central affirmation about the church. It is that community of people who know who they are because they know who their Father is. Their mission is to let all men know who they are. Though there are different interpretations of what makes up the visible church, most Christians would agree that it is "a congregation of faithful men in which the pure Word of God is preached and the sacraments be duly ministered according to Christ's ordinance." And its mission is to proclaim the Good News to the world.

The Mission and the Ministry

In order that this mission may be carried out, Christ has given a ministry to the church. It is his ministry carried out by all the members of his Body, the church. By virtue of their baptism into his Body, all Christians have been commissioned to carry the Good News to the world where they are.

Certain members of the laity (from *laos*—the people) are given authority to carry out specific tasks within the total ministry. They are commissioned to perform special functions on behalf of the entire church, essentially to preach the Word of God and to administer the sacraments. This is a ministry carried on by those members of the church who are ordained for this purpose. The task of these ordained ministers is to help the other members of the church—the lay members—carry out their ministry in the world. The mission of the church is always outward-looking, to carry God's reconciling power to men in the world. It can be said, therefore, that the purpose of the ministry is to help the church be the church in the world.

The ministry is always Christ's. He was given his ministry by God. To carry it out, he came into the world, lived, died, and was raised from the dead, thereby revealing wholly and completely God's love for the world and for the people in it. His resurrection showed that God's Spirit is more powerful than the spirit of separation and that the final answers to the perplexities of men always are on the side of life and love and victory over sin and suffering and death. The ultimate triumph is God's, and it is reconciliation.

Before that is finally accomplished, however, the day-by-day battles continue. The spirit of separation still fights against the spirit of reconciliation. This is the battleground where man finds himself today; it is out of these continuing struggles that his questions arise; and it is here that his decisions for living are made.

Through the church Christ's ministry is now available to help men. It is to bring to the world today the same spirit that Christ brought, the same power that Christ brought, the same love that Christ brought.

As Christian people respond to the Spirit of God in their personal lives they continue Christ's ministry because they are participating in his ongoing work of reconciliation. Every decision, for example, for hope rather than despair is a victory for the power of God and a defeat for the spirit of separation. Every act of personal sacrifice helps release God's Spirit a little further into the world. Every word of forgiveness aids the forces of reconciliation. It is with this spirit and with its power that Christians carry out their ministry in the struggles of life. Indeed, it is in the very struggle that Christians make sense out of life and declare that history is important because it is always God's history and that he is still working out his purpose of reconciliation in it.

Of course, there is no simple solution to the complexities of the human situation and there is no absolutely clear-cut division between Christians and non-Christians. Yet the Christian maintains that the Christian interpretation of history makes more sense than any alternative world view; that the Christian story best describes what life is all about; and that the Christian is committed more to entering fully into living in human history here and now because his acts are a part of God's continuing act of reconciliation against all the powers that separate.

This brings us, finally, to the task of the ordained minister. His ministry is Christ's ministry, given him by the church. His task is the same: to reconcile men to God and to one another. This he does through the exercise of the preaching and sacramental functions of his office and by the witness of his own life.

As God's representative, given the authority of the church, he carries on God's reconciling work. The Good News of the Gospel is that God in Christ has set men free from the power of sin and death; so the central task of the minister is always a setting free of men from the power of sin. Whether this is done by preaching or in pastoral counsel or in a sacramental office, this "absolving power" of the ministry is the key upon which all else rests. The underlying purpose of the ministry is this setting free of men so that they may know themselves as children of God, brothers of one another, and followers of that most Free Man, Jesus Christ.

As Christ took our human life upon him, so are ministers to participate in the lives of those to whom they minister. The ministry cannot be carried out simply from on high, behind a pulpit only, or before an altar. It must be lived among the people where they are. So ministers are the "men-in-the-middle" who are willing to be engaged by life—and by the good, evil, noble, miserable, intelligent, stupid, proud, humble people who make up life.

Their task is to meet people where they are and to help relate them to God. It means meeting them in the midst of their human perplexities, helping them to ask the right human questtions, and bearing witness to the God who alone can provide them with answers adequate for life. This is the task of reconciliation.

It was a ministry to people that Christ carried out. That has been the mark of his eternal ministry for every age. It is only to that kind of ministry that men are ever called. Christ came from God to touch people's lives, to strengthen them, to reconcile them. It is exactly the same today: men deciding for the ministry to touch people's lives, to strengthen them, to reconcile them.

So we can turn now to look at some of the men who are considering this ministry today. By comparison you may be helped to determine whether you should count yourself among them.

The Purpose of the Parables

this with respect is usually the way with the Lord's own
disciples.

Hastily in the night, Joseph, then a man, can escape, first, the
plot and his very thing, second, because you will in a few
days and at the day, for now the other which is neither its
plan in the religion, it's here, the desire, to it of his thoughts in
words. To bring out in a few out into the deep into
whatever purpose it is, to bring out the gap upon the same
set of what it has to set a name of the Lord.
religion full at the place, its teaching so precise, his faithful
the true life of the which should keep deeply sealed so the

3

Who Should Consider
the Ministry?

Two of the men were friends in college. During their senior year they had been asked by the chaplain to consider the ministry. They did, and reported back to him, "No thanks, the ministry is not for us."

Some time later a recruiting agent for General Electric asked them to consider its two-year training program. Shortly thereafter they accepted the invitation, and after graduation embarked on the program.

At the end of the two years they had been introduced to most of the departments: publicity, accounting, technical operations, sales, and all the rest. By that time, as one of the men later reported, "I decided that I didn't believe in refrigerators—at least not enough to dedicate my life to them."

So he went into the office of the recruiting agent, and reported that he was going to resign. The agent pointed out what a promising future lay before him and what a mistake he was making by such a hasty decision. The man replied that it was not hasty but had been in the back of his mind for at least two years. The agent asked what he was going to do.

"I am going to seminary," he replied.

"Seminary? What's that?" the agent asked. So the man told him, and went off to seminary.

A few weeks later his friend, having gone through the same process and having come to the same decision, went into the recruiting agent's office and substantially the same conversation took place. At last the agent asked him what he was going to do.

"I'm going to seminary," he replied.

The recruiting agent's supervisor was in the office at the time. He turned to him, and commented, "My, you certainly are doing a fine job recruiting for G.E."

"Well," replied the agent, "at least they aren't going to Westinghouse!"

"This is where I started from. It was nothing. I had no religion, no faith, no home, nothing.

"All I had was a friend. It was through him I came to believe in a personal God. It was through him, and, to a lesser degree, through others. If I understand anything of what it means to be accepted by God, it is because I was accepted by that friend. If I know God forgives me and loves me, it is because that friend listened to me, was patient with me, hoped for me, and had faith in me.

"He taught me by his example to have a high regard for humility, for charity, for everything that seemed contrary to the standards most people had. Through him I found my way and I found myself and was at last free to make my own decisions. He made it possible for me many years later to promise to follow Jesus Christ. So I became a Christian. Later I became a minister, and the strange thing is that this probably isn't what he intended at all. This is how I began."

"The three of us knew one another well at school, and we entered college as roommates. There was much similarity, as well as diversity, in our backgrounds, skills, and interests. The nature of our friendship was such that we were able to share intimate emotional experiences with perfect frankness if we felt moved to do so.

"One evening one roommate and I went to hear a clergyman who was holding forth on the campus. This clergyman was advertised as being more than happy to handle all intellectual hand grenades that students might wish to toss at him. We armed ourselves accordingly and went to hear the man. At the end of the evening this clergyman singled me out, and invited me to coffee and further discussion the following morning. I can hear my friends' words now—'Pin him down, old man! Make him lay it on the line! Let's get to the bottom of this!'

"Without going into my conversion experience, suffice it to say that he laid it on the line, and I got to the bottom of it with more dispatch than I had bargained for. When I returned to my room and my inquiring roommates, I was in the position of finding it almost impossible to believe that I could no longer disbelieve. The dialogue went something like this:

" 'Well, what happened?'

" 'I don't know.'

" 'Well, what did you find out?'

" 'I found out that it's true!'

" 'That what is true?'

" 'That God really *is* God.'

" 'What does that mean?'

" 'I'm not sure. All I know is that before I didn't believe and now I do.'

"That ended the conversation.

"The important thing was that they could accept this statement of faith although they could in no wise share its conviction. The same is true even today. They believe in the genuineness of my belief while being totally unconvinced of its truth."

A lawyer returned to his pew in church one Sunday morning. He had just received Communion and was waiting for the rest of the congregation to go up the aisle to the altar. It was apparently an endless procession. He became restless and looked at his watch. To his annoyance he saw that he had already been in church for an hour and a half. He looked up at the altar and saw the clergyman pass down the altar rail, distributing the bread, and then go down the rail again, administering the chalice to the same people. He said to himself, "That poor fellow up there needs some help." Then the thought occurred to him, "Perhaps I ought to be up there, helping him."

At that moment he began to consider the ministry; and ten years later he entered it.

The quarterback on the football team was standing under the shower. The water was beating on his back and pouring down his legs. He threw his head back and let the water hit his face. He heard a voice next to him, "Hey, Jack, what are you going to do with your life?"

He looked up, shook the water out of his eyes, and saw it was the end coach. "I don't know," he replied. "Why do you ask?"

"Well," the coach said, "I just want to be sure that you don't sell your soul down the river."

"What do you mean?"

"You'd better take a look at the ministry before you get out of here."

With that the quarterback put his head back under the shower. At that moment he began to consider the ministry.

A department-store executive was seated at his desk on Monday morning looking at the balance sheet from the previous week. It showed a deficit in red. He knew that this week he would have to cut costs to the minimum, sell as much merchandise as possible, and make the balance sheet for the next six days end in the black.

It was an hour before the opening of the store. He walked

out onto the main floor and watched a painter standing on a stepladder, painting the balcony of the floor above. As he watched, the ladder slipped, and the painter fell fourteen feet heavily upon a counter. As the manager ran down the aisle he said to himself, "If that man has damaged any merchandise, I'll kill him."

It was not until that evening, driving home, that he realized what he had said. He apparently was more interested in a profit-and-loss statement than in a human life. That evening, for the first time, he began to consider the ministry.

The thirty-seven-year-old business executive sat down in his study. His wife came in and asked, "Yes, what is it you want to say?" The four children had been put to bed and he had said that he wanted to talk with her.

"Dear," he said, "I'm all through with this business."

"Why?" she said. "What's happened?"

"Nothing's happened."

"Everything is all right at the office, isn't it?"

"Yes, everything is just the way it's always been at the office."

"Did Mr. Brown say you were unsatisfactory?"

"No, he said I was very satisfactory."

"What's the trouble, then?"

"I don't know, but I'm all through. It's a dead end. I've run out of gas."

"Well, what are you going to do?"

"I don't know, but . . ."

"But what?"

"But I'm thinking of the ministry."

"You're thinking of the ministry? How long has that been on your mind?"

"Oh, I don't know. Twenty years, I guess. A fellow at a summer conference once said, 'Joe, have you ever thought of the ministry?' and I said, 'No, I never have.' 'Well,' he said, 'think of it sometime.' And you know, that thought has been nagging me ever since. I think I've got to consider it now some more. What do you think?"

"What do I think? Gosh, I don't know. The ministry? I never in my wildest dreams thought you had that on your mind. I really don't know. But you have to decide. It's your life. But the ministry! Wow!"

"I've always been interested in people. I've always wanted to know what makes them tick For some reason or other, wherever I've been it seems that people seek me out to tell me their troubles. Sometimes I've been able to help them. And that has given me the deepest satisfaction I've ever had.

"First I was premed—until I flunked quantitative chemistry twice. Then I was a psychology major. I think I've been exposed to the principal theories of human behavior and been able to get some insights from most of them.

"For a while I thought seriously of becoming a clinical psychologist. But the more I thought about it, the more it seemed to me that that approach left something out. The clinical approach is concerned about man only as he is and how he can best adjust to the situation he finds himself in. Well, I don't disagree with that, but I was looking for something that would take a man beyond that and point him toward something further down the road. You can call it a search for purpose, or goals in life, or development of a creative spirit, or something like that. The main point is that there is something beyond adjustment and meeting life as it is. It has to do with making more out of life and doing something creative with it.

"So I kind of backed into the ministry, I guess, because it was only at this point that I began to look around for something more than psychology. I see that what I am most concerned about is what religion has always been concerned about, so I felt I had to give the ministry serious consideration. I've still got plenty of doubts, the Lord knows, but I think the general direction of my interests and those of the Christian religion are pretty much the same.

"The things that have challenged me most in college had to do with the life of the intellect. I've been excited and stretched and pulled as I never thought possible by most of the courses and by many of the teachers.

"I learned, for example, that if you are an educated human being you are supposed to have some interpretation of history that is your own. You may be dead wrong, of course, but the point is, you get excited about Marx one month and Spengler the next and Toynbee the third. I'm pretty fuzzy about my own interpretation, but it does seem that there is some principle at work in history, some pattern that fits the rising and the falling of cultures and civilizations. Some people, of course, believe that this is God's eternal purpose, and—who knows?—maybe it is.

"Anyway, I was struggling with some of these ideas in a seminar one day, and afterward the instructor asked me if I'd ever thought of going into the ministry. As a matter of fact I once had when I was about fourteen, but I thought I had outgrown it in college.

"But with that instructor's suggestion I began to go to chapel again. The more I heard the college chaplain, the more I saw that he had a consistent point of view he was trying to present. He had a framework of reference that gave him a leverage for the interpretation of history in general, including our own society and its problems, and for help in personal living. The more I listened to him, the more it seemed to make sense rationally. At least I learned that if you were going to be a Christian, you didn't have to put your intellect in cold storage. The chaplain, in fact, insisted that just the opposite was true and that you had to love God with all your mind.

"The upshot of the whole thing was that I figured I did have to consider the ministry. And that's just what I'm doing now."

"I haven't really the faintest idea how to tell anybody why I am considering the ministry. All I can say is that as I look at most of the men at my college—they're lost. They are just poor, lost, wandering souls who don't know what it's all about. They go back and forth responding to the next pressure that comes down the line, whether it's another drink or a new course or another girl or just sitting around and griping. They don't know which end is up, and when they get through here they'll go to graduate school, or most of them will, just because that's the next thing to come along, and they'd like to duck the draft. Then they'll go to work for their old man or somebody else's old man or some big outfit that takes their old man's place.

"They'll do all this because they won't know what else to do. It's like I say, they're just lost souls—most of them.

"So am I. I'm just as lost as the rest. I don't know what's going on either. That is, I don't really know. I'd like to know. The only thing I've got that most of them don't have is that I know I'm lost. I know it and I don't like it.

"So I'm searching. That's why I'm looking at the ministry. God knows I'm not proud of myself, and I don't think I'm going to bring much to it if I go in.

"But that's neither here nor there. The point is, a lot of these men are just wandering around not knowing what they're looking for. I'd like to find out myself so I could go live with them and say: 'Let's see if we can find home. I'm not sure where it is or how to get there, but I know we've got one.'

"So that's why I am taking a look at the ministry. Maybe I'll find out the answer."

These are some men who have considered the ministry and have decided to enter it. Some of them were young when the idea of the ministry was first presented to them; others were middle-aged, and older. Some had just been graduated from college; others were well established in their business or professional life. Some were bachelors, while others had families. They were all kinds of people, from a wide variety of backgrounds, who made the decision to enter the ministry for any number of reasons.

It may be that one of these situations describes your case. Perhaps you can say of one of them: "There, that's just about where I am now," or, "That's the kind of experience I know about myself." If that is true, then you would be justified in at least considering the ministry. No one can tell another man whether he should be a minister or not. Only you can make that decision. But if any of these examples ring true for you, now is the time to give the matter some careful thought.

Probably all you need do for the time being is to put your considerations in the back of your mind and let them sit there. At the beginning keep your thoughts pretty much to yourself. Indeed, at this juncture it is probably better to talk to no one— or at best to one or two trusted friends. Let the considerations simply grow quietly within you. The time for speaking will come later. For the moment, silence and thinking and considering promise most.

It may be, however, that none of these illustrations speaks to your condition. Let us then press on a little further with specific suggestions that may help you decide whether even to consider the ministry.

The Kind of Person

You should consider the ministry if you have:
 Some faith in God
  Some concern for people
   Some regard for yourself.

These are not requirements for the ministry. They are attitudes. They represent a total point of view that a person has toward life rather than a fixed position. They are not so much minimal standards as they are a way of thinking, feeling, acting. They have to do with the spirit of a person rather than with his technical qualifications.

This section deals with the fundamental question, "What kind of person are you, anyway?" If you are this kind—that is, one who has some faith in God, some concern for people and some regard for himself—then you are the type of person who should consider the ministry. Let us then look at the spirit of such a man.

Some Faith in God

To have some faith in God means—on the broadest possible base—that you are genuinely concerned about what is true. You come sooner or later to recognize that the only important, fundamental question in life is not "How can I succeed?" or "Where will it get me?" but "Is it true?" If it is true, then you have to abide by it. If it is false, you have to repudiate it.

On this level, therefore, you may be critical, questioning, probing, seeking, concerned with a rigorous examination of everything in heaven and earth to discover what is true. While you are not unmindful of the place of sentiment, feelings, and emotions, you seek to put your ultimate faith in truth rather than in subjective feelings.

You take seriously, therefore, the world of ideas. You do not have to be an intellectual but you do get excited sometimes about certain ideas. There is a contagious enthusiasm about ideas that is communicated to people, and, if you are fortunate, you have been imbued with this enthusiasm by a teacher who has himself been possessed by that spirit.

In your response to ideas you keep trying to put various pieces of truth together. You keep searching for some universal principle that holds all the pieces together. As a result you have an open rather than a closed mind. You take it as a mark of intellectual maturity that you remain open always for more truths to be revealed. You consider the closed mind the refuge of either second-rate minds or frightened people.

Along with this search for truth you are not ashamed to confess the mystery that is involved in life. You therefore tend to be humble rather than arrogant before this mystery, and about the truth you know. Indeed, the more truth you receive, the greater the mystery appears. Whether your understanding comes through a deeper awareness of the mystery of nature or the mystery of men, your response has an undercurrent of wonder about it. You may marvel at the power of the atom, or at the resiliency of the human spirit under suffering. In either case, mystery is affirmed and wonder expressed.

In your own personal life this may come into focus in brief, fleeting experiences where you are confronted by mystery suddenly. It may happen as you lie on your back at night on a camping trip and look at the stars; as you are stretched flat on your stomach on the bow of a sailboat that rises and falls with the movement of the water; as you sit under a tree and hear the wind come and go through the branches above; or simply as you examine the intricate and delicate design of a leaf. In any case the world of nature reflects mystery, and somehow that mystery impinges upon your own life. (Or you may have none of those experiences; they are not central.)

Along with this concern for truth and the sense of mystery, there is also a willingness to believe that there may be a relationship between truth, mystery, and life. In precise religious terms this is a willingness to entertain the notion that God is the author of truth and mystery and life; even perhaps that he has brought them together in the person of his Son who is truth incarnate.

It probably, however, will not be nearly so precise a conviction as this at this preliminary stage. There may be no more than a sense of awe before truth and mystery, and a suspicion only that somehow the mystery of life in general and your life in particular will be worked out as that truth and mystery continue to be revealed to you.

One final characteristic is that you are willing to make a decision on the basis of what you do know and to try to live your life in accordance with what you believe to be the truth. You recognize that faith is always a gamble because it is based upon a decision in the face of the unseen and the unknown. You realize also that that unseen and unknown are revealed only to those who commit themselves to it so you are under no illusion that the way to truth is to stay uncommitted, uninvolved. You know, on the contrary, that all truth—even the most "scientific" truth—is revealed to him who is willing to take a gamble that something or some action is "true."

Somewhere in your reading you may have underlined the words of Anselm, "For I do not seek to understand that I may believe, but I believe in order to understand." [1] You have in your own personal experience discovered that this kind of commitment is the only way by which love and friendship are given. You may indeed be beginning to wonder if further knowledge of the universe does not rest upon your being willing to trust that universe by making the affirmation of faith that God is truth; that at the heart of the mystery of truth is love; and that you are called on to commit yourself to whatever it is that you know to be true.

In a very general way these are the qualities of mind and spirit that reflect a breadth and depth consistent with and pointing toward faith in God.

---

[1] Anselm, *Prosloquium,* Chap. I (Open Court, 1951), p. 7.

Some Concern for People

To have some concern for people means simply in the first instance that you like to be with them. You are happy, for example, to go to a ball game with some friends, not simply to watch the ball game, but just to be with friends. You are not intent either about giving anything or receiving anything. You are just happy that they are and that you can be with them.

The wider the range of people that you like to be with, of course, the better. To search for and cultivate relationships with all kinds of people rather than simply your own kind you consider to be a mark of growth and maturity.

This tendency is not unrelated to the search we discussed above: seeking some universal truth that will hold all differing bits of truth together. Here on the personal level you search for the thread or common spirit that binds all men together. You try to establish mutuality, and as large a corporate life as possible, rather than dividing people into exclusive cliques or fragmented groups.

This spirit may be found in your concern for the odd duck who is never really accepted by any group. The fact that he is not accepted makes you uneasy. In certain moments of courage you are willing to leave your group and go identify yourself with him. You know it is important for people to feel accepted, and sometimes you are willing to go out of your way to accept those who have been rejected.

This may mean that you want to "help" people. Possibly you find that your own deepest satisfactions are related in some way to making some contribution to the lives of others. You discover sooner or later that this does not rest upon your feelings or your likes and dislikes. There are plenty of people whom you do not like emotionally and yet you still have a desire to be of service to them. You want to try to establish them as fully as possible as human beings by accepting them simply as they are. Later you may discover this is not far removed from Christian love.

This attitude may be expressed in your concern for social issues in the community where you are. It may be manifested in identification with community causes, help with the "neediest cases," or support of social work. It may center around discrimination because of race in a school system, or with selectivity and rejection within a fraternity system.

In any case, you are concerned about people not only on the level of personal friendship but also in the larger framework of community and group living. You may find yourself thinking of service in the State Department or with the United Nations or with some other enterprise that promises hope for a world where men may live together with greater justice and brotherhood.

Finally you are aware that embedded in the heart of all personal relationships based on love and friendship, as well as in all corporate relationships based on justice, there is some structure of right and wrong. You appeal to it; you try to abide by it; you encourage other people to abide by it. The values of right and wrong are significant.

You recognize by your study of history that these standards of right and wrong are relative and that they change from culture to culture. The important fact, however, is that there is always some standard of right and wrong. You therefore find yourself searching for some universal criterion by which standards may be evaluated. It may be that in this search and response to understanding you come to believe that right is important not simply as a means toward an end but as an end in itself. It may come to you, for example, in your wrestling with honor and dishonor on examinations. You may realize that honor is important, not because it can be used to make a better society or to make people better, but because it is in itself a proper end. You want to be related to it simply because it *is*.

So much, then, for some of the general attitudes that have a bearing upon your concern for others. In sum, you find within yourself a tendency (not always felt and not always expressed) to wish your fellow man *well*.

Some Regard for Yourself

This means that you want to have your life count for something. You suspect that it will be able to count only in relationship to something more than yourself. You are not content to find meaning for your life simply in terms of your own success or your own wealth or your own prestige.

You have—perhaps hidden in the secret recesses of your mind—some high sense of what life is meant to be. It is not simply for your own life but for others' as well. You have a picture, only dimly perceived perhaps, that life is meant to be affirmed and that there must be some quality of greatness about it. You are, therefore, impatient with shoddy, debased ideas of human enjoyment and human destiny.

This is not to say that you are not aware of your own limitations. Indeed, it may very well be that in the face of this high regard for yourself you have a deeper sense of your limitations than you would otherwise have. You know that you are not what you ought to be, and you have no illusions about being protected from temptation. You have undoubtedly succumbed to temptation—perhaps in every area of life. Nevertheless you are not overly cast down by this. You know that you have a best self that is expressed when it is caught up in concern for others, and perhaps also in those moments when you are alone before God. You many even suspect that somehow there is a relationship between your going out to people and being before God.

You are willing, therefore, to be involved with people, and, if it seems appropriate, to be involved with people and God. You may not be at all clear about the latter, but you are not ashamed about your interest.

You find within yourself a desire (sometimes strong, sometimes weak) to live in accordance with what you believe to be true about God and man. Although you fail many times, there is underneath an intention that your life shall express your honestly held affirmations about God, about people, and about yourself. You want to live in accordance with your own deepest convictions.

It may be that these convictions have come to you within the life of the church—and it may be that they have not. The church may not now speak to your condition in any precise or affirmative fashion. Indeed, you may be very impatient with the church.

On the other hand, it may be that the church has always been important for you. You discover that what you understand about God and about people and yourself began and has matured precisely because your life has been within the church. Therefore in order to be true to yourself you are also true to the church. This means your participation in the life of the church is in accordance with what you believe God wants you to do.

As far as preliminary considerations are concerned, then, what is important is the style of living that you express. What kind of person are you? What are your general attitudes toward life? What do you think about God and the universe and man? How do you tentatively look upon yourself as you move ahead into life?

Here are some questions you may ask yourself:

Do you find yourself dissatisfied with making money as your chief goal in life? Are you bored with the goal of a secure, though uninteresting, job? Do you ever wonder why God permits so much suffering in the world, especially among people you know who are good people? Do you think that there may be justice on the side of the underdeveloped countries in Asia and Africa in their rebellion against the West and the white races? Do you feel somewhat guilty? Do you wish you could do something about it?

Do you have at times a genuine desire to be of service to mankind in general or to some individuals in particular? Do you get annoyed with the students who won't give to the Campus Chest because they "don't believe in charity" but who will spend one hundred dollars on a week-end date? Do you find yourself tempted to do the same thing?

If you give your word to do something do you make a real effort to keep it? Even if it turns out to be to your disadvantage? Are you willing to flunk an examination rather than cheat? When you have a date do you make any effort to see that she has a good time? Even more than that you do?

Do you have some sense of compassion for the odd fellow on the campus who doesn't make any fraternity? Do you ever go out of your way just to say "hello" to him? Have you been more concerned to establish understanding of truth (or behavior) that will include rather than exclude people? Would you rather vote people into a club or blackball them to keep them out?

Do you have some sense of the power of the unseen in life? Do you believe that "seeing is believing" is inadequate as a basis for living? When you are able to do the right thing does this make you happier than doing the wrong thing? Have you ever wondered why at times it is so much more fun to do the wrong thing? and still done the right? Do you once in a while have the sense of being in God's presence and wanting above all else to do his will? and finding in it a peace and joy that never quite come in any other way? [2]

If the general trend of your answers to these questions is affirmative rather than negative, you have good reason to believe that God may be calling you to the ministry. In any case, you can be certain that you would be justified in keeping the idea

[2] These questions are suggested by a passage from F. D. Maurice, *The Kingdom of Christ* (Student Christian Movement Press, 1958), II, 109.

of the ministry in the back of your mind until you are ready later
to make a firm decision on the basis of further study and inquiry.

A Word of Encouragement

You do not need to have:
    Absolute certainty about God
      Complete love for everyone
        A perfect life of your own.
These considerations have to do with the beginnings. They
are concerned with the direction in which you are facing as you
begin your journey rather than with the attainment of your
destination. They are not conditions for considering the ministry but guides for your thinking.

Some Objections Considered

If you are going to consider the ministry, you will at the very
beginning want to consider some of the objections to it. They
usually center around four important areas.

1. "I am not good enough."

This is a perfectly proper and natural objection because it
reflects first of all an honest appraisal of oneself. The fact is
that no man is "good enough" to presume to be able to speak
in behalf of God or to be of help to men.

Second, it reveals also an awareness that the Christian life does have within it an ethical rigor and that values are an important part of Christian behavior.

On the other hand, this type of objection reveals a popular (and profound) misunderstanding of the essential nature of the Christian faith. Generally speaking, in our culture Christianity is equated with morality. The "Christian man" is considered to be the "good man." On one level Christian behavior is interpreted to mean one should not smoke, not drink, and never dance. It is made up of prohibitions against the natural human enjoyment of life, and seems to imply that the Christian life is a denial of life.

Ethics and morality are an integral part of the Christian faith, but Christianity does not begin there. Christianity begins with what God has done in Christ. There is in Christ the act of God's love toward all men. Even though we are unlovable people, we are forgiven by God and brought back into a relationship with him. This is the Good News: not that we first loved God, but that he loved us.

The point here is that we are all forgiven, although not one of us is "good enough." No Christian ever declares that he has become so good that he is worthy of God's love. He confirms not his goodness, but God's.

Therefore to say "I am not good enough" may very well be the first sign along the road that leads to the ministry rather than an obstacle that prevents one from going there. No man is good enough in himself to minister to people in the name of God or to receive God's love. And that is precisely the point. How one behaves—one's moral and ethical life—is therefore always in response to what God has done. It is always the second step, the human reply to God's initiative. The central Christian affirmation has to do with God's continuing love for us. Morality and ethics follow from this. The equation that morality equals Christianity is dead wrong.

2. "If I join the church, do I leave the world?"

This question is sometimes put like this: "Can I be a minister and still be myself?"

It focuses attention upon the relationship of the church to the world. The church does not exist in order to snatch people from the world so that they may become safely protected from the world. It exists, on the contrary, for the purpose of helping people enter into the world and to live their lives in the world more fully, with enthusiasm and power.

Even those churches that provide ministries for men and women to withdraw for a life of prayer and contemplation do so in part "for the sake of the world." It is felt that the life of prayer may be, for certain ones who are called to this special ministry, the most effective way by which they can make their contribution to the world.

So the answer to the question is: No, you do not leave the world. God so loved the world that he sent his Son into it. Christians are sent into it and ministers are sent into it. If it is right for you to be in the ministry, you can be certain not only that you can be yourself but also that you can come to your best self there.

3. "How can I be sure?"

The first comment to be made is that you do not, at this juncture, have to be sure. As a matter of fact it is probably better for you not to press to try to be certain now. There is no need for you to decide immediately.

All that is required of you is that you respond to God where you are in the way that you believe God wants you to respond. The story of your life is written chapter by chapter. The source of great difficulty for us is that we often try to write the fourth chapter before we have finished living the second. Our only task is to complete each chapter in life as it comes. Then when we finish one chapter, we will know how to begin the next.

Since we are now only "considering," the important attitude is to remain open to the possibility of the ministry. To make a final decision—either for or against—early in one's consideration is almost always a mistake. It is generally premature and therefore immature.

One way of realizing this is to remember that the ministry is not crucial in itself. *God* is crucial. *You* are crucial. If you keep that relationship clearly in mind, and live in accordance with it, then the decision for the ministry may come as a necessary response on your part to God. Let it come, however, in its own time.

4. "But I haven't been 'called.'"

When a person makes this comment he usually is thinking in a very literal fashion of a voice "calling" him or a vision appearing before him. He probably has in the back of his mind the picture of God calling the little boy Samuel after he had gone to bed, and Samuel, finally, after assistance from Eli, answering, "Speak, for thy servant heareth."

Now, it is perfectly true that some men have an experience of such emotional content and power that they can only describe it in just such terms as these. It is as though a physical voice spoke to them or a vision objectively appeared.

One man, for example, tells of his walking through the deep snow after listening to a meditation given during a retreat in a little mountain village. "I was making my way slowly across a field where the freshly fallen snow came up almost to my waist," he said, "when suddenly I felt a sudden urge to pray. So out there all alone I knelt down. With one part of my mind I felt foolish and with the other part I was praying as hard as I ever had in my life. Then it came to me that I had once and for all to face God and to come to grips with him. This conviction came to me with such intensity that I would have sworn I heard a voice saying, 'face up,' though of course I knew there was no such voice outside me. It was rather a shattering inner conviction that seized me."

The key phrase here for most of us probably is "it came to me." We have all had experiences where suddenly we realized a truth that had remained hidden up to then. We say "it broke upon me" or "I saw the light." We may have been struggling with the issues involved for a long time. Then they all fell into place at once, and we had made a discovery.

So a man might say, "Finally it came to me that I was in love with Mary, and that I had been for a long time without knowing it." Or a person might say, "One day it came to me that I was the one at fault, that I had been wrong all the time; and then I had to ask for the other's forgiveness."

In other words experiences such as these that have great emotional intensity may constitute a "call." They come at a time of great crisis or when there has been a long period of emotional ferment under the surface. They are experiences related to all aspects of life, however, and are not necessarily distinctly religious in nature.

Only a minority of men who enter the ministry today have such experiences. Valid as they are, and representing honest human situations as they do, they do not constitute the normal way by which men decide for the ministry today. Experiences such as we have been considering are determined by a man's temperament, emotional life, background, and education. There will, therefore, be a wide variety of such experiences, all of them subjective and of critical importance to the person involved. They do not, however, represent effective, external, objective criteria to help other people make a decision either for or against the ministry.

The majority of men decide themselves. They decide under God, which means that they make their decision in faith. But it is their decision. They make it, finally, because they want to —and in the long run there is no better way.

You never can be "sure" until you make the decision. And even then there well may be some lingering doubts. That, after all, is part and parcel of what it means to be a free human being: to have freedom of choice, to decide—and then to reflect about it afterward.

So the problem here is just the same problem that is presented to any human being faced with any choice—to be a doctor or teacher or clerk in the post office. It is the same problem that faces a man when he chooses a wife. The point is that you *can* choose any one of several girls, but you choose one. You can't be sure she is the right girl until you make your decision—and even then you may have some doubts. The choice, however (with her help), has been yours, and the mystery and grace involved in that decision and commitment are part of what it is to be a man.

Your decision for the ministry is, in somewhat the same way, the choice you make with God's help. This is to make a decision in faith. It is not, however, meant to be in blind faith. It is meant to be in intelligent faith so that your decision can be an intelligent one. The purpose of this book is to help you make your decision for or against the ministry an intelligent one.

If you now use your mind, as well as you are able, to examine the ministry carefully and thoughtfully, and if at the same time you live your life under God as honestly as you know how, then in God's time you will be able to make the decision about the ministry that is right.

There may be many things about the Christian faith and life you cannot be positive about, but about this you can be dead certain.

4

Can a Life Committed
to the Contemporary
Church Count?

THE PURPOSE OF THIS CHAPTER IS TO DEAL AS HONESTLY AS
possible with one of the obstacles presented to men considering
the ministry: the institutional church. It is often not so much a
lack of faith in God that prevents a man from deciding for the
ministry as it is a lack of confidence in the church.

Thoughtful men who are genuinely concerned about the relationship of the Christian Gospel to the contemporary world
and who look seriously and critically at the church frequently
reflect attitudes ranging from uneasiness through impatience to
despair. They are not at all certain, as they observe the actual
situation in the church today, that they would be justified in
identifying themselves with it as ministers, and many decide
that their lives will count for more as Christian lives if they
work through other, apparently more significant organizations.

The question "Is this where my life can count for most
today?" reflects a more fundamental question: "Does the church
count for much in our society today?" Is there any evidence
that the church makes any critical difference in our culture at
all? It is to these question that we now turn, and we can best

do so by first facing frankly the major weaknesses of the institutional church and then examining some of its present strengths.

Weaknesses of the Church

1. The church is no longer central to society.

The days when society consisted of farming communities that centered upon homes on a village common dominated by the church spire are gone forever. The church no longer is in the center but has been edged out to the periphery of society. It is dominated by apartment houses, office buildings, and factories —especially factories, because they have now become the special symbol of our society. They have not simply surrounded the churches; they have hemmed them in. Sometimes they have strangled them, cut them off not only from air but also from people.

Many times, along with their people, the churches have fled to the suburbs; there is more air there. Indeed, there they have taken new root, found better soil, and have flourished. Statistics of church growth are most impressive. Approximately 60 percent of the population declare they belong to some form of organized religion.

But in the flight to the suburbs the churches have left society behind. The suburbs where the churches flourish are where America eats and sleeps and plays. It is in the cities that America *works*. And in a working society that is industrialized the church has lost its place. It has much to say about what goes on in the homes where families are, and in part in the schools where their children are taught, but in the industries where people work it has nothing to say. The real world in our culture is the industrial world, and here the voice of the church is not heard —because it does not know what to say. When it does speak it uses a foreign tongue that is seldom understood.

This general observation is so universally true that it need hardly be described, much less debated. The fact is that the world (for this is far larger than Western society) is in the midst of an industrial revolution that began at the end of the eighteenth century and is simply gathering momentum.

Industrialization has brought in its wake two forces that have greatly affected the church: urbanization and mobility. It is estimated that two out of three Americans now live in the city and that the average citizen moves once every five years. The impersonal nature of city life and the impermanence of residence have brought into being a generation of people on the move who do not become deeply involved in either personal or community relationships.

The urbanization of our society and the mobility of its population have brought a sense of transciency and anonymity. The church has been able to survive best in those areas, largely suburban, where the *domestic* life of the family is carried on. The meaning of the Christian faith, therefore, has been interpreted in large measure in terms of personal living. It has been concerned—and quite properly—with the values of family life, the meaning of Christian marriage, the Christian nurture of children, and other issues that center upon interpersonal relationships. As a result, the life of the church has been built primarily around the lives of the women and children, for they are the ones who are in the suburbs twenty-four hours a day.

The men are in the city working. They are working in a world that is in the midst of a technological revolution. Whether as executives or as laborers, their work is increasingly impersonal and fragmented. On the higher levels executive decisions are more and more group or committee decisions and less and less individual decisions. As one young executive put it: "The orders are given to us now by a committee. Every order comes from 'them' rather from one man to whom I am responsible. When things go wrong 'they' get blamed. No longer is there very much of the man-to-man relationship." This depersonalization is of course even greater on an assembly line where a man has a responsibility only to a machine to see that it functions properly. The human element—including both the ability to create and the freedom to make mistakes—is kept to a minimum.

In this society where man *works,* the church today has no place. Perhaps it would be clearer to say that there is no conscious relationship between a man's Christian personal life and his working life. It is not so much that his working life is un-Christian or anti-Christian as it is that adjectives like "Christian" do not apply. He is involved in earning a living, and it does not occur to him that there is any element about it that is either Christian or not Christian.

So far as the fundamental structure of our society is concerned, the place of the church is on the edge. It plays no significant role in those areas where decisions that affect the life and destiny of whole peoples are made. Whether it is in the choice of new products a company will produce, the percentage of interest charged on mortgage loans, the kind of aid to go to underdeveloped nations, the type of tariff reductions, hourly wages paid to migrant workers, regulations on stock exchanges, control of public transportation, selection of automobile models or new fashions—in a word, wherever contemporary man *works* —what the church says or thinks makes no difference to anybody.

*2. The church follows, rather than leads,
society.*

Traditionally the church has been a conservative force in every society; it has usually tended to identify itself with the *status quo;* the institutional side of the church inevitably develops a stake in maintaining a stable structure of society.

Yet there has always been within the Judeo-Christian tradition another side, which has been called the prophetic element in religion. The task of prophecy has been to "discern the signs of the times," to see what *God* is bringing to pass as the history of peoples and societies unfolds, to point to the judgment he brings upon all institutions, including the church institution, when they are obstacles to his working his purposes out, and to encourage the forces in society that promise greater justice and brotherhood so the corporate life of peoples may be carried out more in accordance with his will.

The church in the West only infrequently honors this prophetic tradition today. To illustrate with one obvious example, it takes no great discernment to recognize that there is a worldwide people's revolution under way. There is a tidal wave of upheaval against the old society and the structures that society had built. This is seen in the universal revolt against every form of imperialism and colonialism. In the past sixteen years in Africa, to take but one area, there have been established twentyfive new nations. Both Africa and Asia are in ferment, and one of the central points at issue is race. The revolt of the colored races against the white race throughout the world is one of the most clear-cut "signs of the times."

One would think that the church, charged with a prophetic responsibility, would speak and act clearly and without equivocation on this issue and would provide Western society with the leadership it needs (and indeed expects) from the church. This leadership has not been forthcoming.

To be sure, every Christian church has spoken about the equality of races and the need for brotherhood among all men. But in the only arena that counts—the arena where people live and meet each other—the church has not shown the way. Leadership on this issue has come instead from purely secular forces in our society. The Armed Services have shown greater courage and initiative in breaking the barriers between races than have the churches. The church on the local scene, in other words, has lagged behind society. And even today it is still probably true that "the most segregated hour in America is eleven o'clock on Sunday morning."

Little wonder, then, that many men concerned with how they can best serve God and man today question if greater opportunities are not provided outside the organized church than within it. There is an appeal presented by such organizations as the United Nations, the Peace Corps, the State Department, and countless others that without any pretension simply declare that they have important work to do for the sake of mankind and want men to do it. The organized church has in general failed to present any similar challenge for men to provide leadership to society on moral or ethical issues.

3. The church is overly preoccupied with itself.

No one who examines a local congregation carefully today would suspect that the primary reason that the church is organized is for the sake of the people who do not belong to it. Most of the evidence points directly the other way.

The church, however, was brought into being by God's Spirit

in order that the Good News of what God had done in Christ might be proclaimed to all peoples. This outward-looking direction is where the church faces when it understands that its primary central task is its mission to those who stand outside.

Yet it is in practice an inward-looking organization, especially on the level of the local church. This is simply to say that most of the time, energy and money spent by the organized congregations of the church are spent on themselves.

This general picture is seen in detail when one examines almost any area of church life. To turn only to finances, forty-nine Protestant and Orthodox churches in 1960 received from their members $2,407,464,641. Of this amount, $428,591,000 was spent for "benevolences," and $73,267,000 for foreign missions. This was 17.8 percent of the total giving; or, for every dollar spent on those outside the church approximately $5.00 was spent on those inside.[1]

The organizational life of the church reflects the same emphasis. An untoward amount of energy is expended by women's organizations, for example, on rummage sales, Christmas bazaars, clothing exchanges, and the like. To be sure, much of this money is devoted to good causes, but anyone who has ever been involved in this side of church life knows that what is really important is the enlisting and holding of the interest of the women who already belong to the church rather than any overwhelming concern for the missionary enterprise.

The situation is the same in sections of men's work within the church. "Give the man a job, and you have the man" is the slogan. This is sometimes difficult when there are not enough jobs to go around and when few of the jobs tax a man's abilities. One clergyman proudly stated that he had the problem of men's

[1] *Year Book of the American Churches for 1962* p. 271. A notable exception: in 1962 the Park Street Church in Boston had a general budget of $105,950 and a mission budget of $280,000.

work solved by the organizing of an ushers' corps. "We now have eighty-six men enlisted to do regular duty," he boasted. When asked how often a member of this corps would actively usher, he answered, "about 2.5 services a year"—hardly a noble challenge to Christian discipleship.

The role of the minister in such a congregation is primarily to serve as a chaplain to those who are already members of the church. His ministry is almost exclusively a ministry to the "in-group"; and giving proper adequate pastoral care to them taxes all his resources and time. Clearly these are the people to whom he has been sent to minister, and it is essential that they receive the best he has to offer. Exclusive emphasis upon this side of his responsibilities, however, makes it impossible for him to devote adequate time or thought to what is equally his task: to be a bearer of the Good News to those outside the church. He is meant to be not only a chaplain, but a missionary as well.

This is one of the reasons, for example, that the church so infrequently ministers in any significant way even to its immediate community. The minister's task is thought of as ministering to church members, most of whom may, in certain places, live miles from the church. He therefore is unable to identify himself with the local community and its problems. Yet this is what must be done if the church is to serve those who stand outside it. A church that does not carry out its mission to the world where it is will ultimately wither and die.

The Methodist Church's Convocation on Urban Life in America, for example, recently reported "that unless the urban church could adjust to the sweeping changes in modern city living it would die. . . . There was general agreement that the city church could no longer afford to remain aloof from its environment. The summation emphasized that this would entail close cooperation with community movements, aimed at easing race tension, participation in inter-faith projects and the establishment of special ministries and services for residents of any faith or no faith." [2]

Concentration upon its own inner life tends, therefore, to develop a "church world" that is set apart from the "real world." In this "church world" there is a wide range of activities and services, opportunity for recognition and personal satisfactions, for which all church members are eligible. The danger, of course, is that church people will spend more and more time in this world and less and less time in the other world. The religious world is thought of as a "better" world, and communication between the two worlds becomes increasingly difficult. The division between the Sunday activity of church people and their weekday activity becomes complete, and except for those who give themselves full time to the "church world," the division is carried on within the lives of the members themselves.

The "church world" develops its own religious language, which is unlike any tongue people in the "real world" speak. It is concerned with religious experience, whereas contemporary man is more interested in human experience. The preaching tends to be moralistic and sentimental; it is frequently no more than exhortation to be good; or it consists of ineffectual homilies about trivial matters. There is little evidence of God's Word preached with power and authority and the conviction of a reasoned faith. The services as often as not are either centered on the personality of the minister or in a rigid ritual that seems unrelated to anything significant in the lives of people where they are. The worship of God, therefore, in many places is insipid, flat, and removed, with the members of the congregation spectators rather than participants. Seldom is there any vital sense of the presence of God in the services of worship, with the joy and power that always go with that presence.

All this points to one final description of what happens to the people of a church overly preoccupied with itself. They be-

[2] *New York Times,* Feb. 23, 1961, p. 32.

come to all intents and purposes "practical atheists." This is not to say that they do not believe in God. They do. Every research poll ever taken on this subject reveals that the vast majority of Americans—let alone church people—believe in God.

But the God they believe in, in the words of J. B. Phillips is "too small." [3] He is "the man upstairs" who stands watch over his people, ready to be called on for their slightest need (described by someone as a "celestial bellhop"); he is the God captured by the confessional statement of some church, and therefore he becomes "our God"; or he is the God who is revealed in some sacramental structure, and he belongs to all those who belong to the same structure.

In any case this God is not the God of Abraham, Isaac, and Jacob who himself directs all history—including twentieth century history—and who takes the initiative to choose us rather than our choosing him. He is not *really* regarded as the sovereign God who is at work in the cold war and the advance of communism and the struggle for integration and the unfolding of the mysteries of space. Nor is this God the one who at the same time is personally interested in me and my family and my job and my next paycheck.

Our God is "too small." So for all practical purposes it can be said that many of the people of the organized churches do not really believe in God.

4. The church is divided.

"The scandal of division" is in the eyes of the world inexcusable. And the world is right.

The "scandal" is clear on at least two counts, one theological and the other practical. The first has to do with the clear

[3] J. B. Phillips, *Your God Is Too Small* (The Macmillan Company, 1952).

Christian affirmation that all Christians are members of the Body of Christ which is the church, that there is one Body and that Christians are therefore members one of another. The simple historical fact of the matter is that, in contrast to this, the church is visibly divided, and some branches of the church have been and are now set against one another.

The practical concern is set forth by the man in the world to the church with his question: "Why can't you fellows get together? I don't become a member of the church because I can't make up my mind which church to belong to." Christ put this practical matter in his prayer to God "that they all may be one . . . that the world may believe that thou hast sent me." [4] The mission of the church is weakened beyond measure by its present divisions. The clear call to be a Christian becomes muffled when it must be hedged about with denominational restrictions—with, for example, some of those set up by the two hundred and fifty-nine church bodies in the Protestant church in the United States.

However important and understandable it was for Christians in the past to be set against one another because of their concern for the Gospel and passion to witness to their differing interpretations of it, that day is no more. The issues that were of critical importance then are of less importance now—of almost no interest to the man in the church, and of absolutely none to the man in the world. The disunity of the contemporary church is one of its gravest weaknesses, and its mission will continue to be relatively ineffective as long as disunity continues.

So much, then, for a description of some of the weaknesses of the organized church as they appear not simply to the critic who stands outside the church but also to many of its critics who stand inside and love it. Now let us, without minimizing the seriousness of anything that has been said above, turn to examine the strengths of the organized church.

[4] John 17:21.

Strengths of the Church

*1. The greatest strength in the
contemporary church is its recovery of its
sense of mission.*

By this is not meant a determination to give more money or
men to the missionary enterprise; nor is it to declare again that
the church has a mission; it is rather a realization that the
church by its very nature *is* mission. That is to say, when a
person is called to be a Christian he is at the same time *sent*
to be a Christian. There is, in other words, a new sense of the
critical importance of the relationship of the church to the
world and of the task of what it is to be a Christian in the
world. The emphasis has been changing from "join the church
and leave the world" to "be the church and enter the world."
Signs of this change have begun to appear in many areas of
the church's life and it is some of these we shall now examine.

Nowhere has this change been made more evident than in
new understanding of what is meant by the ministry. One way
to understand this is to distinguish between the words "vocation" and "ministry." The former means "calling" and the latter,
"service."

All men are "called" by God to a personal relationship with
him. This calling (vocation) is essentially the same for everyone. The meaning of Christian vocation is that we all are called
to repentance and faith and to a new life with Christ within the
fellowship of the church. We are all called to this life in order
that we may help the church accomplish its mission in the
world.

How we perform this service is our ministry. We are called
to serve God (to exercise our ministry) in different ways.

It follows, therefore, that ministry is the service of all of the people who are called into the life of the church—not just the ordained clergymen. The ministries in this sense are varied and many. There are as many ministries as there are ways of serving. Christians may minister as teachers, insurance salesmen, plumbers, doctors, railway engineers, architects, or clerks. Women may serve as secretaries, wives, mothers, schoolteachers, models or taxicab drivers.

This means, of course, that lay people have a ministry. This ministry of the laity is of crucial significance in the world today as it is the primary means by which the mission of the church is carried out. Men and women who have a sense that where they are is where God wants them to be and that what they are doing is the way by which they may serve him and their fellowmen have a very high sense of the ministry. The ministry, then, is always the ministry of the church—the ordained and the lay people together—because the ministry is always the means whereby service is performed, service of God and man.

This ministry, as we have seen in Chapter 2, is Christ's. As all the members of the church perform their ministry, the church is able to carry out its work for Christ in the world.

Christ's ministry is to the world. As layman and minister alike share in that ministry, then to that extent the mission of the church is being carried out. This is the central emphasis: Christ presently, actively, quietly through Christian people wherever they may be in the world accomplishing his mission. The church, the ministry, the mission, its people—it is all of a piece. This recapturing of the sense of mission is the main strength of the contemporary church, and it is also its greatest hope for establishing a stronger relationship to the world.

Part of the new understanding of the mission of the church is seen in the interest in Biblical theology, which describes how God acted in the events recorded in the Bible, and affirms that the Christian faith has to do, first, with what God has done and continues to do, and then with the response that man makes. It is seen also in part in the revival of interest in what has come to be known as the liturgical movement, the key mark of which is the active participation of the laity in the services of worship by their presenting the offering of their work to God, thus signifying the close relationship of work and worship. A third evidence of the concern for the church's mission is found in what may be described as renewal through small groups. In them, men and women wrestle with the fundamental question: What difference does it make to be a Christian where I work?

In such ways as these there is a new expression of concern and evidence of strength in the church for the resolving of the fundamental issue of the relation of the church to industrial society. They represent the probing, questioning, searching that is an absolute necessity if the issue is ultimately to be resolved. It is at any rate clear that increasing numbers of Christian people know that they have a critical responsibility to be engaged in this world's work as Christians, to be involved in the day-by-day decisions that every man must face, and to carry out so far as they are able their understanding of what the mission of the church is.

That task has been described by Hendrick Kraemer in these words: "Unselfish and disinterested service to fellow men in numberless forms, often without uttering one so-called 'religious' word; being reconciler in the grievous conflicts that separate men and communities; questioning the world incessantly and inducing it to put the *right* questions in regard to its problems; letting itself be questioned by the world, contradicting it when necessary, and reminding it of the divine judgment which hangs over everything and everyone; throughout all this service—reconciliation, contradiction and questioning —sounding the note of the certainty of God's triumphant love." [5]

[5] H. Kraemer, *A Theology of the Laity* (Westminster Press, 1958), p. 186.

So this spirit of renewal is fostered by every effort of the church to establish and maintain communication with society. It is seen in industrial chaplaincies, team ministries, store-front churches, retreat and conference centers, and in every other expression of that spirit of concern that comes best through committed Christian men and women meeting together.

2. The re-union of the church is taking place.

The late Archbishop of Canterbury, William Temple, described the movement of the churches toward reunion as "the great new fact of our day." There can be no question that this fact is one of the moving forces within Christendom, and represents one of the great strengths within the contemporary church.

There also can be no question about where this strength comes from. It arises from the sense of mission of the church, and is intimately related to it. A church that takes seriously its commission to preach the Gospel to all nations finds itself weakened immeasurably by its divided and fragmented witness to that Gospel. It is not surprising, therefore, to see that the most far-reaching steps toward unity are coming from the mission areas. When Christians find themselves a very small minority in a non-Christian land, and are subjected to severe pressures to conform to the standards of the society where they are, they know that they cannot afford the luxury of a divided church.

The most significant efforts toward reunion accordingly have come from India and the so-called "younger churches." In 1948 there was brought into being the Church of South India which incorporated Christians who had formerly belonged to the Methodist, Presbyterian, Congregational churches, and four dioceses of the Anglican Communion. Two other proposals that are now under consideration, and that go even further, look forward to unifying even more churches through what are known as the Ceylon (or Lanka) Scheme and the North India-Pakistan plan.

This is not the place to recount the story of the movement toward reunion.[6] It is enough to say that the first chapter began in 1910 at the Edinburgh Missionary Conference, followed by meetings at Stockholm in 1925 and Lausanne in 1927. A Provisional Committee of the World Council was established in 1939, and then came the formation of the World Council of Churches in 1948 at Amsterdam. The most recent chapter was written in New Delhi in November, 1961, when twenty-three churches, including the Russian Orthodox, were admitted to full membership. There are now 203 churches that belong, representing Protestant, Orthodox, and Anglican bodies. The only major bodies not officially involved in the work of the World Council are the Southern Baptist and the Roman Catholic, although it should be noted that the latter had five unofficial observers at New Delhi. Rome itself has called an Ecumenical Conference, the Second Vatican Council, for 1962.

In the United States the National Council of Churches of Christ in America is made up of thirty-four church bodies that participate fully, and thirty-five that participate in part, representing forty million Protestant and Orthodox Christians.

This is beyond any doubt a day when the spirit of reunion is at work among the churches. This spirit is stronger today than at any time within the past four hundred years, and it is considered by most Christians to be clearly of God. Much remains to be done, and there are serious obstacles that lie along the road to reunion, but this is a generation that will not be

---

[6] It can be read in: G. K. A. Bell, *The Kingship of Christ* (The Canfield Press, St. Albans, 1954); Samuel McCrea Cavert, *On the Road to Christian Unity* (Harper & Brothers, 1961); and Stephen Neill and Ruth Rouse, *A History of the Ecumenical Movement, 1517–1948* (Westminster Press, 1954).

content without further progress toward that goal that "all may be one."

3. The church points to God.

There are clearly many organizations other than the church that are carrying out God's will in the world. Wherever mutuality is established, justice maintained, love expressed, the creative spirit of man set free—as well as in other ways—God is at work.

The church, however, by its very nature, bears witness to God. It may do it well or ill, be a good witness or a poor one, but it always points to God in some way. Its business, so to speak, is making reference to God, and making it clear to men that they cannot in the long run do their business or the business of society without reference to him.

We live in a day when the primary concern of man is man and his life on this planet. The question that intrigues this generation is, What is man? All the resources of human society —psychological, anthropological, sociological, biological, historical, and all the rest—are being brought to bear on this question so that man might have a clearer idea of who he is and what he is here for.

Within all the variety of answers given, the church says that the question cannot be fully answered without reference to God. It does not say that all other answers are wrong, but that they are incomplete without including a religious dimension. The mystery and complexities of the human spirit—what it is to be a human being—are just too great to be accounted for without some idea that man is a creature bound to earth and with a destiny that always transcends the earth and human understanding.

The church, in other words, takes the same question, "What is man?" and says it can be answered only within the context of a wider question, posed first by the psalmist, "What is man, that *thou* art mindful of him?" [7]

The church declares, furthermore, that if a society does not make reference to God as it deals with this question it becomes in effect a godless society, in which the seeds of its own decay have begun. Once a society has no regard for God, then it ends by having no regard for man. The most vivid illustration is provided by the tyranny of Nazi Germany, where there was finally no concern whatsoever for the human spirit, or the dignity of man, or even human life. And it is no accident that the Nazis, while able to take over industry and labor unions and the universities, were never able completely to dominate the churches. Nor is it, by the same token, surprising to see today the continuing vitality and in some instances the growth of the churches in communist countries.

Man can be understood fully not only as a human being grounded in life and history but also as a person whose spirit is self-transcendent and who can be explained only in relation to God who created him.

To keep pointing to God so that men keep looking up is, then, the task of the church. This is one of its strengths. When it is evident that it does this because it is concerned about men as well as about God, the church will become infinitely stronger.

This kind of reference to God is not made by the church to downgrade man, but to upgrade him. Indeed, the point is that man can be fully man only when he understands himself as he truly is—a child of God, created by him to know, love, and serve him and other men. Once he has been grasped by this truth, then he can be himself perfectly freely and without fear. He then has grounds for infinite hope in what he and all the human race can accomplish. His human life is good and important and worth living creatively to the fullest—because it is God's.

[7] Psalm 8:4.

4. The church is God's.

The greatest strength that the church has is God's strength. This is not to say that the church is to be identified with God, but it is to say that the church is the instrument appointed by God to carry out his mission in the world.

To a person standing outside the church this statement will sound either presumptuous or foolish. It is, however, a statement that must be made, for it stands close to the heart of what the church believes, not simply about itself, but about the meaning of history and the human enterprise.

In a word, God called the church into being; he gathered the people together in a common life of faith centered in his Son Jesus Christ; and he gave them a commission to reveal who he was to men so that they would come to know who they were. This is the church's mission; God has sealed it, and he has promised to be with it until the end of time, when he will complete the task.

The people of the church, who are the church, are asked then to bear witness to Christ and to his purpose generation after generation. This means the affirming of God as the Lord of all history and of all life from the very beginning, through the events in which we participate, and so until the very end of time. Men who come to understand who they are under God gather together to worship him, and then disperse into the world to serve him. Their task is to extend in their day the love of God and man. In the mystery of God's Providence he chose the people of the church to do this for the sake of the world that he loves.

Now, the church is not called to be successful in this task. It is called to be faithful. Success will be given it at certain times; at other times it will be a failure. This is not important, nor is it even the business of the church. That is God's business.

The business of the church is to be faithful to its mission given it by God. So long as it does this, then it will have available for its task the strength of God. This is why its greatest strength is God's strength.

In attempting to evaluate the strengths and weaknesses of the church, we can perhaps be sure only of this: God's purpose will continue to be carried out in history, not only in structures and institutions beyond the church but also in and through the institutional church. We can properly be annoyed with the church, provoked by it, exasperated with it. We can do so, however, because we are loyal to it, because it has a special place in God's purpose in the world, and because society expects greatness from it.

God himself will continue to judge it as he leads it. As in other ages, he will come through all the forces of history to refine it, purify it, make it equal to its task. In the meantime we are to be faithful to it. Probably there has never been a time when faithful ministers were needed so much as now to call the church to her central task.

So we can return to the question asked at the beginning of the chapter, "Can a Life Committed to the Contemporary Church Count?" You have now considered most of the evidence that can be presented one way or the other. You are in a position to make some tentative answer to that question. If your answer for the moment is "yes," then you will want to consider more fully what the ministry means.

The only reason for making a final decision about the ministry, however, is not that your life can count here, but that God wants you here. Wherever he wants you is the only place where your life *can* count. So the further question is "How can I decide whether God wants me in the ministry?"

It is to help you come to an intelligent decision about that question that the balance of the book is directed.

5

The Best Preparation for
the Ministry: Life

THE BEST WAY TO PREPARE FOR THE MINISTRY IS TO PREPARE
for life. Whatever helps a man get ready to live as a mature,
responsible, useful citizen helps prepare him for the ministry.

Preparation is preparation of yourself as a person. The root
meaning of the word "parson" is "person." What you are as a
person will in large measure determine what you are as a parson.
Humanly speaking, a man's ministry rests upon what he is as a
man, and the failures that a man has in the ministry are almost
always human failures.

The most thorough preparation for the ministry, therefore,
is thorough participation in the human enterprise. It means entering as fully as possible into those human experiences that
promise growth and maturity—but to enter into them for what
they give now rather than for what they promise to give later.
You enter upon them simply because it is good to be involved
in life, and you are eager to be involved now. All human experiences that help you develop both your freedom and your sense of
responsibilty enable you to live more fully, and will therefore
ultimately be of help to you in the ministry.

In brief, preparation has to do with everything that goes into
making you what you *are*. It has to do with helping you get

ready to live as completely as possible as a human being in the twentieth century. This means in almost every instance college preparation.

Preparation in College

College education should enable a student: (1) to participate in the world of learning; (2) to live in a community where there are rich personal associations; and (3) to be helped to find meaning and purpose in life. These areas correspond roughly with academic, extracurricular, and the religious interests. Any educated man should be grounded in all three areas. To put it another way, no man can be said to be truly educated who has not been possessed in some measure by the world of ideas and responded on his own to seek some aspect of truth, who has not identified himself in some personal way with the members of the human community where he is living, and who does not have some philosophy of life that claims his own personal allegiance.

If these are the marks of educated man, they provide by the same token the best guide by which a man may prepare himself for the ministry. So let us look at each one in turn.

1. The World of Learning

Although it escapes the notice of some students, the primary purpose of a college education is to introduce them to the world of learning and to help them come awake intellectually. When this takes place, they discover that a college experience is worthwhile and indeed worth almost any sacrifice.

Intellectual awakening may come in almost any way and at any time. It may come through an orderly and crystal-clear lecture given by a professor who knows his subject and is enthusiastic about it. It may come as you work on a paper or a thesis. In that preparation you deal with material that you have collected yourself; you put it together in your way, and when it is done something new has been added to the subject. It may not be much of a contribution to the world of knowledge; it may not mean very much to anyone else; but for you it has been an introduction into a totally new and exciting community—the community of scholars and teachers whose only concern is with truth, the search for it, being possessed by it, transmitting it.

This introduction to learning may come as you stand before the test tubes in the laboratory, and at last the catalyst works and you prove the experiment; or as you uncover with your scalpel the arteries of a rat, or see under the microscope the capillaries of a leaf; when you balance an equation or master the irregular verbs. It may take place during an argument when it dawns on you that your interpertation of the Sherman Antitrust Act can be properly defended; or when you are alone, reading Robert Frost's "The Gift Outright" in a corner in the library, and you suddenly see how poetry may be a means of communication and grace. At some moment in some strange way something happens, and previously fragmented bits and scraps of knowledge begin to fall into place.

However it comes to pass, whenever you do become intellectually awake and begin to respond to the whole world of learning, you have begun to be educated. The excitement of dealing with truth becomes yours, and your response will be part of you for the rest of your life.

There are two words that are appropriate here to say to men who are considering the ministry. The first is this: follow your own intellectual interests just as far as you can. It does not make any difference what those interests are. They can be in any field—scientific, philosophical, the humanities, social science. What is important is that you respond as fully as possible in accordance with your own inner drive in response to that aspect of truth that is opened to you. The only limitations should be those determined by your ability.

It may be that you will discover that your intellectual interests awaken your religious interests. The world of ideas is God's world, and from the Christian point of view when one is dealing with truth one is dealing with God. The intellectual path has been for many the way to God—and ultimately to the ministry. It can come in any field and at any time.

One man discovered this in the field of political theory. "I was planning to go into law," he comments, "when I took a course in political theory. There for the first time I came up against the fundamental fact that if you are going to deal with political structures you have to deal first of all with the men who create those structures. This means you have to consider the nature of that man.

"So you read about him. You read Hobbes, Locke, and Rousseau, then Machiavelli. These men all present differing political structures to support society because each one has a different understanding of the nature of man. Is man by nature good, evil, or neutral?

"This fundamental concern about the nature of man rather than about the nature of the state became clearer to me when I took a course in Marxism. Marx has both a determinist and a utopian understanding of man. He is contradictory in his theory of the state because he is confused in his theory of human nature. Then, in trying to work through some of the problems of neutralism in Germany with the rise of Hitler, I was led back to Luther and his position about the powers of the state being ordained by God. This took me, finally, all the way back to Paul. What struck me about Paul was not so much his political theory as a passage in his letter to the Romans:

'For I know that in me (that is, in my flesh,) dwelleth no good thing: for to will is present with me; but how to perform that which is good I find not.

'For the good that I would I do not: but the evil which I would not, that I do. . . .

'O wretched man that I am! who shall deliver me from the body of this death?' [1]

"Paul seemed to me here to get at the very heart of the problem of the state because this is the central problem of man and his nature. His description of man was certainly accurate so far as I read other men and myself: 'For the good that I would I do not: but the evil which I would not, that I do.' When I saw his answer to the question 'Who shall deliver me from the body of this death?' to be a simple affirmation, 'I thank God through Jesus Christ our Lord,' [2] I was finally led to wrestle with the problem of human nature as somehow related to God. This was my introduction on an intellectual level to the Christian faith."

Another man had his religious position developed because in English literature he was introduced to logical positivism. This provided him with a great educational experience. He felt that he was being encouraged to deal only with facts, and to throw out as irresponsible sentiment all that could not be "proved."

"I came to realize," he later wrote, "that this method of analyzing human experience when carried to its logical extreme meant that nobody can say anything. The analysis of words as central to the problem of meaning led to an inability to use any words. The rejection of all experience that cannot be 'proved' brought finally the rejection of every experience that men find worthwhile. The impatience with 'blind faith' resulted in a negation of all faith. That was for me an absolute dead end.

"This approach to learning seems always to bring men to precisely this dead end. It is a refreshing, ruthlessly realistic approach to truth—and it never gets a man beyond his denials. Sooner or later, however, he has to make some affirmations. If

[1] Romans 7:18–19, 24.
[2] Romans 7:25.

he is to make any declaration he has to do so on the basis of faith and decisions. I can only acknowledge an abiding conviction that all positivism is of tremendous importance for clearing out the underbrush in thinking and for clarifying a realistic approach to the facts of life. You are then in a position to take the step beyond and to make some kind of affirmation about the meaning of life, and these are in some sense religious affirmations, because they can never simply be proved by facts."

Illustrations such as these simply point to the fact that intellectual awakening is frequently associated with religious awakening. This is even more forcibly strengthened by the experience of the Rockefeller Brothers Theological Fellowship Fund.[3] This program is designed to offer men who are intellectually outstanding and qualified in all other respects an opportunity to consider the ministry by attending a theological seminary for one year with all expenses paid. Men who have already decided to enter the ministry are not eligible. In the first five-year period after the program came into existence, 65 percent of the men, after this year of study, made the decision to enter the ministry. This is one of the strongest accessions of strength to come to the Protestant ministry since World War II, and its approach is through emphasis upon learning.

The second word for men who are considering the ministry while in college is this: keep your academic program balanced. Any balanced program is one that includes some study in the humanities, natural and social sciences, and in foreign languages.

The American Association of Theological Schools has for many years recommended a course of study for men preparing to enter the ministry. The following statement presents the position of the Association:

It is desirable that the student's work in these fields of study should be evaluated on the basis of his mastery of these

[3] 163 Nassau Street, Princeton, N.J.

fields rather than in terms of semester hours or credits. That this recommendation may help the student faced with the practical problem of selecting courses, however, it is suggested that he take 30 semesters or 90 semester hours or approximately three-fourths of his college work in the following specific areas:

English—literature, composition, speech and related studies. At least 6 semesters.

History—ancient, modern European, and American. At least 3 semesters.

Philosophy—orientation in history, content and method. At least 3 semesters.

Natural sciences—preferably physics, chemistry and biology. At least 2 semesters.

Social sciences—psychology, sociology, economics, political science and education. At least 6 semesters, including at least 1 semester of psychology.

Foreign languages—one or more of the following linguistic avenues to man's thought and tools of scholarly research: Latin, Greek, Hebrew, German, French. Students who anticipate post-graduate studies are urged to undertake these disciplines early in their training as opportunity offers. At least 4 semesters.

Religion—a thorough knowledge of the content of the Bible is indispensable, together with an introduction to the major religious traditions and theological problems in the context of the principal aspects of human culture outlined above. The pre-seminary student may well seek counsel of the seminary of his choice in order most profitably to use the resources of his college. At least 3 semesters.

Of the various possible areas of concentration, where areas of concentration are required, English, philosophy and history are regarded as the most desirable.[4]

[4] The American Association of Theological Schools, *Statement on Pre-Seminary Studies*. There has recently been undertaken a two-year study of pretheological education, with support from the Lilly Foundation, which may result in significant changes in these recommendations and will in any case bring them up to date.

For our particular purpose certain general observations may be made about the fundamental fields of study. It is the humanities that more than any other single area provide the basic raw material with which theological education deals. A student who has been exposed during his undergraduate years to the whole drama of the human enterprise as it has been lived in history, in art and philosophy, in music and literature, in the highest expressions of the human spirit will have the best foundation upon which to build his theological education.

Is it wise to major in religion in college? In the years before World War II and directly following, it was almost universal practice to counsel against this and to urge men planning to enter seminary to major in some department other than religion and so develop a broad educational and cultural foundation. As you will note from the present A.A.T.S. recommendations, this remains the general policy.

No doubt the principle here is a sound one. It is important that pretheological education not be narrowly defined or concerned exclusively with "religion" and "religious courses" but that the widest possible scope of studies be undertaken. If God is truly the God of history, then the best way to be introduced to him and his acts is to see what actually happens on the field of history. If God's Spirit is really the force that dwells in the spirit of man so that he may be creative, then let the student be exposed to music and drama and all the arts. This principle continues to be the proper one in most instances.

There are, however, two considerations that prevent that principle from being absolute. The first is that in recent years departments of religion have not only expanded in colleges and universities; they have also become immeasurably better. The day when a department of religion consisted of one retired minister giving courses in the Bible is gone. The last fifteen years have seen a procession of graduate students complete their Ph.D. or Th.D. programs on a level of excellence comparable with the requirements of any other department. Indeed, in some instances the departments of religion, by providing excellent instruction in the field of religion, introduce students to the humanistic study of man in the broadest sense. It is no longer true that in every instance a major in religion is a narrowing educational experience. Actually, the contrary may be true.

The other consideration applies to men who are planning to go to seminary or to some other graduate school in preparation for the teaching ministry. These men will frequently find it to their advantage to major in religion in college so that they may have mastered the essential body of material by the time they enter seminary. This will apply particularly to those students of outstanding intellectual ability (the only ones who should be encouraged to do advanced work leading to a doctor's degree), but there are enough of them to justify this further exception to the general principle about majoring in religion.

Language study is an indispensable part of academic preparation, and the first step is to learn how to read, write, and speak the English language. Words are the tools of communication, and their proper use is essential. To be able to read with comprehension, to write grammatically and to speak clearly and coherently are the attainments of men who are educated. It is increasingly difficult for a man to graduate from college without having ever studied any foreign language—but it can be done. It is not possible, however, to consider such a man educated. Normally a college graduate should have had a minimum of three years of an ancient language (usually Latin) and three or four years of one modern language (or alternatively, two or three years of each of two modern ones). This is adequate language background for the study of theology, except for the students who are considering further graduate work after completing a B.D. program. Those students should offer as a minimum for graduate study two ancient and two modern languages.

Greek is studied in seminary because it is the language in which the New Testament was written. Requirements for the study of Greek may vary within both churches and seminaries. Ability to use the language introduces one to the "behind the scenes" documents that make up the basic historical records of the Christian faith. Although Greek may always be begun in seminary, and is required for admission in relatively few, it is desirable to have some introduction to it in college.

The study of some natural science is required for most students for graduation from college. We live in an age when the appeal of natural science is great and when men qualified educationally are promised the highest material rewards that a scientifically-minded society can offer them.

It is, therefore, all the more important that men who are considering the ministry undertake some firsthand study of natural science and participate with some thoroughness in the learning process in accordance with the "scientific method." The gap that exists between the humanities and the sciences can be bridged only by those who have some understanding of the two disciplines and who have themselves been educated in both fields. Some study in such fields as physics, chemistry, mathematics, or biology is essential.

Since the social sciences have as their primary concern the study of man, they also provide an important part of pre-theological education. Some work in anthropology, political science, psychology, sociology, and economics is thus highly desirable.

2. A Community of People

A balanced college program means not only a balanced academic schedule but also a proper balance between intellectual and other interests. The cultivation of friendships with students and teachers from a wide variety of backgrounds is one way by which this takes place. There is a cross-section of mankind on a college campus that is unique in American life. There are intellectuals of every description whose interests range from atheism to zoology; some are people of wide culture and catholic taste; others are single-minded enthusiasts who have concern for nothing beyond their special field. To be exposed to all sorts and conditions of people, and then to develop deep friendships with a few of them is one of the most enriching experiences of college. Friends are gifts of grace of great price, and provide an important complement to the academic life in college, to say nothing of what they mean in later life.

The other way by which balance is provided is through participation in extracurricular activities. The "learning process" is engaged in on the athletic field or in the office of the college newspaper as surely as in the classroom. A certain humility that comes in no other way is given you when an effective block takes you out of a football play; existential truth that does not come through books is conveyed when you are jarred to the marrow of your bones. In athletics you learn, for example, that positions of leadership, such as team captain, are usually given, not necessarily to the best player, but to the most dependable one. Doing the best with what your native athletic abilities are is more highly regarded than having outstanding skills. It is the everlasting keeping at it—showing up for practice on time every day, practicing hook shots with your left hand if you can already do them with your right, working on grounders if you have no trouble with fly balls—that pays off in the long run. In Christian terms this is referred to as fidelity; it is seen by any athlete who has eyes to see.

Responsibility for college publications, participation in social organizations, involvement in other interest groups—all provide important experiences for growth. There is value in working one's way in part through college, quite beyond the monetary value. In short, a variety of experiences means the stretching that is necessary if maturity is going to be a natural part of college education. The extracurricular activities provide some opportunity for "learning by doing," and the principle of participation is a simple one: follow your own interests as far as you can without getting them out of balance in relation to your total college experience.

3. Religious Life

If a student is responding to his college experience by engaging seriously in the intellectual life of the college, or some part of it, and by participating in some measure in the community life beyond the classroom, then it is inevitable that he will begin to form his basic philosophy of life. He will unconsciously accept certain norms of behavior as proper for himself; he will examine many sets of values and select some; he will adopt some interpretation of the meaning of his own life and relate it in some way to a sense of ultimate meaning in the universe, which may or may not include some specific religious reference; he will make clear what that means by the decisions and choices he makes in his life. In a word, if a man is being educated he is inevitably adopting some code of behavior and some philosophy of life that best express what he is as a person. That is, in effect, his religious faith.

a. RELIGIOUS ACTIVITIES

The immediate question now before us is, "To what extent does participation in religious activities help a college student in his education and in his intelligent consideration of the ministry?" On some campuses association with the organized forces of religion will provide immeasurable help in coming to know

God and man; on others, such associations will only confine and restrict that knowledge. The mark that distinguishes one from the other appears to be the degree to which religious groups are concerned with the total life of the campus or only with the "religious" life. If it is the former, it is healthy; if it is the latter, it is sick.

Probably the strongest religious activities program is one in which participation is open to all members of the campus and yet which is directed by an inner core of students committed to the Christian faith. This type of organization welcomes men of varying religious convictions or with no convictions whatsoever. Its aim is to be inclusive rather than exclusive. It provides opportunities for service by carrying on social-service enterprises, work with young people in the community outside the college, directing summer camps for the underprivileged, assuming responsibility for the Campus Chest, and other activities of this nature. It also organizes informal study groups where students meet with a member of the faculty to study particular aspects of religious faith. There will be loosely organized Bible study and prayer groups, and some ordered worship in accordance with a commonly accepted religious tradition. Its social outlook will always be related to the concerns of the men and women on the college campus. It will, therefore, take the initiative in dealing with such moral issues as discrimination. It will accept seriously its responsibility to relate those issues to continuing Christian traditions and to make clear the relevance of the Gospel on the campus for that generation.

Where these conditions exist in any appreciable measure, opportunity for religious growth is offered to college students because there is opportunity for human growth. Religion is related to life; there is freedom to accept one another as persons without insisting on agreement of beliefs; and there is opportunity for conviction to be expressed without compromise.

On the other hand there are religious organizations that are primarily exclusive. Membership is limited to those who hold a common religious belief; the subjects for discussion are almost always "religious" subjects (as though God were more interested in religion than he is in life). There tends to be an undue emphasis on "religious" activity (frequently upon the ceremonial aspects of worship activities); the "table talk" is often primarily ecclesiastical gossip; and the spirit of the group is inclined to be set "over against" (and therefore "better than") the spirit of the college. Generally speaking, no useful purpose—either educational or religious—is served simply by belonging to such a group. The image of the ministry that is unconsciously given is that of withdrawal from real life to participate in church life, and it does not appeal to men who are genuinely concerned to minister to people where they are. The only value in identifying oneself with this kind of religious organization is to work from within to break down its exclusive character and to open it up to the serious challenge presented to it by the college community. Indeed, this would be a ministry in itself, and may be the most effective way by which some students can serve God on their campus.

b. Religious problems

The typical religious problems that arise on a college campus are no different from those that arise anywhere. They are seen in sharper focus sometimes, however, because the college years are a time of rapid change in the development of a student's personality. They not only are years of rapid physical and intellectual growth; they are also years when most students for the first time are given the freedom to strike out on their own. Their passage may at times be a very turbulent one. Let us then look briefly at certain key problems, at least for the purpose of identifying them.

The fundamental problem is the problem of *authority*. The

most important gift that is given to all college students is freedom, and for many of them it is the first time they have known any real freedom. They are free of the authority exercised by the family and by the church; they are free from a schedule that controls every waking hour; during the first months they are free of any judgment from any authority until examinations are given. One college dean concluded his welcoming address to the freshman class with these words, "And now you are free to do anything you want—provided you don't get put in jail." That is a wider range of freedom than most freshmen have been accustomed to.

How a college student deals with authority and freedom determines the progress of his education, for there can be no education without freedom. Freedom is prevented from turning into license when a man decides under which authorities he will place himself. Growth, in other words, revolves around his wrestling with the authority problem.

The most obvious illustration is provided by the way in which a college student handles the authority represented by his family. For some, college means an opportunity to repudiate that authority entirely; for others it is a more gradual emancipation. In either case education means developing the ability to come to decisions of one's own. Those decisions may or may not be consistent with decisions made by the parents of the student, but they will not be made simply because of parental authority.

Thus in many instances the student, in his struggle to become a mature, responsible adult will find himself rejecting the religious ideas of his parents—not necessarily because he believes the ideas are wrong in themselves but simply because they are those of his parents. It is important for him—if he is to develop any religious faith of his own—at times to stand apart from the religious faith of his family.

In such cases as these, parents who attempt to exercise their own authority do nothing but raise obstacles to the student's free development. College chaplains every year receive letters from distraught mothers saying in effect: "Johnny no longer goes to church. What shall I do?" The answer is: "Nothing. Anything you do directly will cause only damage. What you are called on to do is to remain faithful to your own religious conviction and bear witness to that. Then in time Johnny will come to his own position. He will now be most strongly influenced by your example—never by your authority."

The same reaction is seen in those instances where a student comes from an authoritarian church. If he has been brought up in a church tradition that has emphasized authority— whether Biblical or ecclesiastical—and he has been taught that all religious truths must be "taken on faith," he will inevitably react against this. Education is concerned with the development of a man's mind, the cultivation of reason, and the sharpening of his critical faculties. This is not to say that reason alone is the guide to living for the reasonable man. It is to say that this is the instrument it is the purpose of education to strengthen and refine. No area of life—including the area of religious faith— should be exempt from its scrutiny. This is the only way by which a reasonable faith may be developed and by which the educated man may become also a religious man.

To hold that religious authority is above reason or against reason is to cause a man who is being educated to rebel against it. This repudiation may be so violent and emotional that it may be years before he is able to examine religion in a reasonable manner. Many of the professors who are "campus atheists" are those who in their adolescent years rebelled against the authority of religion and have not been able even as adults to come to terms with it on any rational basis.

To deal seriously with the intellectual challenge to the religious faith is an important function of education. It may be bewildering for a student who has, for example, been taught that

God literally created the world in six days to discover that geologists believe that life took at least five hundred million years to evolve. This is precisely the kind of struggle, however, that provides intellectual stimulus and in the long run develops a mature religious faith. It is the very heart of education.

Religious ideas will, therefore, be expected to change. Sometimes it is the *religious* duty of chaplains to stimulate these changes that there may be growth. This can only be done as a man is set free from false ideas that restrict and confine—especially false ideas of God. At times drastic action may be needed, as the following example illustrates.

A college student had announced when he entered college that he intended to go into the ministry. One evening as a junior he shared with the chaplain his misgivings about that decision.

"I'm scared," he said. "I promised God once that I would go into the ministry, and now I'm not so sure."

"How did that happen?" the chaplain asked.

"Well," he replied, "I told God five years ago that I would go into the ministry if he would bring back my older brother alive from Korea. We had received word that his plane was downed somewhere. That's when I made that promise to God. Then six months later we learned he had been picked up by the Chinese and was in prison camp. When the war was over, he was released and came home. Ever since, I've had this sense of commitment to God, but now I have lots of doubts about my own religious faith and I'm getting so I even hate to go to church."

The chaplain spoke: "Look, brother, you don't have to hold to this agreement with God. You tried to make a bargain with God that if he would do something for you, you would do something for him. This isn't the kind of God the Christians worship. He is a God who loves you and wishes you well no mattter what you're like. He didn't bring back your brother alive *be-*

cause you made that promise to him. All he wants you to do is to respond to him as fully as you can as a human being. Maybe this means the ministry and maybe it doesn't. But he doesn't want you to go into the ministry under coercion, and certainly not on the basis of an idea you had about him when you were fifteen years old."

"Well, what do you think I'd better do, then?" the boy asked.

"If I were you I would drop all religious activity for a while. Stop going to church. What do you like doing best, anyway?"

"I really would like to spend my extra time with the dramatic outfit."

"Well, then, go do it. Go be yourself for six months and see what happens. At the end of six months come back and we'll talk about it."

At the end of six months the man did come back, and they did talk about it. A year later he made the decision to apply to seminary. This time, however, he did it freely and upon his own. He did it because he wanted to, and not because he had to. It was therefore a responsible adult decision.

The key to the problem of religious authority for the under-graduate rests, then, upon his use of freedom and his willingness responsibly to accept certain authorities for his own. This is seen in such obvious matters as normal participation in the life of the church. Once the first heady sense of freedom has subsided and he begins to come to grips with the truth repre-sented in religious faith that is expressed in some organized structure, the question of denominational loyalty arises.

The principle that offers the best promise for growth rests upon a *grounding* in one denomination, and an *expansion* into an understanding (and appreciation) of others. The grounding will give you roots and the sense of stability that comes from belonging to one particular group of God's people. The counsel of Baron Friedrich von Hügel, a Roman Catholic layman, to people who were tempted to become Roman Catholics was always to stay where God had placed them (by birth or circumstances) unless and until they came to believe it was a sin for them to stay there. Put as strongly as this, it discourages the casual and superficial moving from denomination to denomination, or from one preacher to another, and stresses the importance of stability for religious faith to be nurtured.

At the same time college does provide an opportunity for new ecclesiastical horizons to be explored and for new understanding to be appreciated. It is altogether proper, therefore, to become exposed to religious truth as apprehended by traditions other than one's own, and to participate, as far as one can in good conscience, in those other activities and worship. One is called always in the religious life to that challenging—yet finally the most creative—task of remaining loyal to the truth one has already received and at the same time remaining open to truth that is yet being revealed.

The final expression of the authority problem is seen in that arena where all problems—including religious ones—are revealed and sometimes resolved: life itself. All problems become problems of living, and religious decisions become decisions about how to live. The central question becomes: By what authority do you make your decisions in your everyday life on the campus?

This question may in turn be divided into two parts: (1) How do you respond to academic authority? and (2) How do you respond to the authority of the crowd? The first point can be made very simply: your life as a student is expressed as you study. The purpose of going to college is to learn, and how well you discharge that responsibility is determined by how well you apply your native resources to the task at hand. Your vocation, in other words, is essentially to be a student, and your religion is revealed in part by your response to academic authority. Indeed, the vitality of your religious conviction will often be expressed more honestly in how you respond to your studies than how you participate in "religious" activities.

The second point has to do with your response to the pressures exercised by your contemporaries—the authority of conformity. The need to be accepted and to belong to a group socially approved in any environment and culture is recognized as one of man's basic social needs. The necessity and desirability of this is not at issue here.

What is at issue is this: How do you maintain your own values when they are in conflict with the values of your contemporaries? How do you hold onto your own integrity when you are under pressure to violate it? How can you be at the same time true to yourself and also acceptable to the accepting group? Are you a moral chameleon who develops the art of protective coloration, so that your values shift as you move from group to group? Or are you a man who tries to stand firmly on the basis of his own inner convictions?

The fundamental problems that have to be wrestled with in this area of living do not change greatly from generation to generation, although their forms may vary. There is always, for example, the elementary issue of simple honesty. Does cheating on an examination hurt anybody—especially if everybody else is doing it? There is the issue of discrimination. Is not the choice of one's friends a basic human right? If some people want to make choices automatically on the basis of the color of skin or race or religious affirmations, is not this perfectly natural? Is not drinking simply a matter of social custom and personal taste? So long as I don't hurt anyone, whether I get drunk or not is nobody's business, is it? With regard to sexual morality, isn't the best guide determined by what social custom is? Isn't the philosophy behind the statistical reports really the most reliable: what is statistically most frequent is most natural; what is most natural is most human; what is most human is most right?

These are some of the perennial problems that appear on a college campus, that deal with living issues, and about which students are making decisions day by day. They all reflect the basic problem: By what authority are you going to make your decisions? Will it be your own or will it be the group authority?

One of the difficulties for any student genuinely concerned about this problem is that he feels that he stands alone. The fact is, of course, that there are many who share his convictions, but he does not know it. One student made the comment to his college chaplain that he was dead set against the blackball system in his fraternity, but that he was the only one in the fraternity who felt that way about it, and what could he do alone? The chaplain had had two other students from the same fraternity say precisely the same thing to him previously. He put the three men in touch with one another; they presented their case to the fraternity; and at the end of the year the blackball system was killed.

The traditional Saturday-night fraternity beer-drinking sessions with dates from a neighboring college were changed in one month by the chance remark of one girl to her date at the end of such an evening. "I won't be back next week," she said. "I'm sick and tired of being a female occasion." He responded by saying that he was as bored with the tradition as she, and why didn't they do something about it? As a result, on alternate Saturday nights some of the men and their dates took under-privileged school children in town on roller-skating expeditions.

Once a man is willing to stand up and be counted on any of these issues, he almost always finds that he does not stand alone and that others will rally to his support. But whether they do or not, he has acted on the basis of his own inner convictions, and that is what is important.

Whatever the issue, and however you meet it, it is there that your religious faith has bearing. The decisions you make as a member of the college community concerned about all sides of its life will reflect your basic religious concern. The best possible preparation you can have for the ministry is the preparation provided by living as fully as you can in the college community. If the decisions you make there reflect your most honest conviction about those living issues, then you will be able to make the right decision about the ministry, when the time comes for that decision to be made.

After College—What Step Next?

Should a college graduate go directly to seminary or should he make a definite break by working or by military service?

In general a man who has clearly made up his mind for the ministry should proceed to take the next natural step and go to seminary. If you have made this vocational decision, have had summer jobs outside the academic environment, and are regarded as a reasonably mature and balanced individual, then there is no reason why you should delay. This is particularly true if you are an outstanding student and are considering the possibility of doing further graduate study after you have completed seminary.[5]

There are generally two classes of men who ought not to go directly to seminary, although there are so many exceptions in both groups that any general statement is open to serious question. On balance, however, you probably ought not to go directly to seminary if you are (1) immature or (2) the son of a minister.

(1) If you are immature and inexperienced and have not

---

[5] The degree programs most frequently taken beyond the B.A. and B.S. levels are as follows: Bachelor of Divinity (B.D.) or Bachelor of Sacred Theology (S.T.B.)—three years; Doctor of Theology (Th.D.)—two or three years after a B.D.; Doctor of Philosophy (Ph.D.)—two or three years after a B.D., or, alternately, three or four years after an A.B.

faced any of the realities of life except those found in academic communities, you should interrupt your studies before proceeding. There may be no real question about your decision to go into the ministry ultimately, but if all you know about life is what has come to you through "book learning" it is important for you to get some knowledge about life by living with people.

To take some time out after college in order to enter into some of the normal living human experiences of people, may, therefore, be the best step for you to take. One of the difficulties in seminary revolves around men who are not prepared emotionally for the ministry, although they may be very well qualified academically, just because they do not know very much about life.

There is no human experience or work that cannot be entered into as proper preparation for the ministry. For men who have not been exposed to the rigors of life outside an academic experience, an "interim period" can be turned to profitable use. Almost any work experience—particularly if it puts him in touch with people—will do. The raw material of human experience gained in secular work will provide him with a richer and rougher personality to be educated in seminary.

(2) If you are the son of a minister—particularly if you are the son of a *successful* minister—you probably should defer going directly to seminary from college. The son of a clergyman has so many unconscious pressures to live with that it is exceptionally important for him to be certain that his decision to go into the ministry is his own free decision.

No psychological test has yet been devised (nor will be) to illumine perfectly the dark areas of human motivation. It is difficult to discern the reasons for behavior in the heart and mind of another; motivation for the ministry as for other decisions is almost always mixed; there is an ambiguity of good and evil in most human decisions.

What is beyond question, however, is that so far as possible a man should have *his own* reasons for his basic decisions in life. He should go into the ministry only because it is something he wants to do, that he believes is right for himself—and not in response to pressures from outside.

It is exceedingly difficult for the son of a minister to do this until he has had an opportunity to stand on his own two feet outside the ministry. Clergymen seldom try to persuade their sons to follow in their footsteps. Indeed, they usually lean over backward not to do this—so much so, in fact, that that extra "permissiveness" in itself becomes all the more subtle and persuasive as an influence. A man's own integrity becomes one of the "hidden persuaders" of the spirit. It shows what a great mystery spirit really is.

In any case, ministers' sons almost always profit by separating themselves for some interim period of time from the normal progression from college to seminary and then to ordination and the ministry. Either a secular position or military service provides in the space of two or three years sufficient time for a young man to become sufficiently disassociated from his family so that he may take an objective look at the ministry and then make his own mature decision.

The Question of Military Service

The one common fact of life that all college seniors must deal with in one way or another is military service. What is the responsibility of the man planning to enter the ministry toward this fact?

Legally there is no question about it: there is no responsibility. Under the present Selective Service Regulations any man enrolled in a properly accredited seminary preparing for the ministry is exempt from military service and is given a classification of 4D by his draft board.

Morally, however, the issue is not so clear. It has to do with whether the exception granted by the government is morally a right or a privilege. It is complicated by the fact that a man who intends to minister to a generation has a particular responsibility to be identified with that generation. In this age the one common factor that most young men in American life have to deal with is military service. Some men preparing for the ministry, therefore, consider that they have a particular responsibility to be associated with their generation in discharging this responsibility—else they would be unable to minister to them effectively later. Other men do not accept this position, believing that the moral issue is not at all clear, and that they have no responsibility beyond that required by the laws of society, which have provided for exemption.

Military service is urged by many on the psychological grounds that it provides a maturing experience for men—particularly if they have been protected during their academic life. It is certainly true that military service does expose one to a wider cross-section of mankind than usually appears on any campus. Military service itself, insofar as it provides discipline and the sense of being under authority, may be a strengthening experience. There is no guarantee, however, that this will be the case. Many men do not find that the military service matures or enriches them but rather regard it as a waste of time. There is nothing automatic about virtue being given through military service alone. The value rests largely upon the motivation of the man who participates in it. If he goes into military service only "to get it over with," that is all that happens. He finally "gets it over with." If, however, he enlists in order to identify himself with a human experience typical of his generation, to relate to as many different types of men and experiences as possible, then he is given an almost unparalleled opportunity to grow. Part of this motivation may be simply a desire to serve his country on the grounds of patriotism, a not unworthy and not unusual reason.

Inasmuch as the advantages and disadvantages of military service rest so largely upon the subjective, personal motivations, it is impossible to draw a general conclusion. There is, however, one absolute that can be presented to every man considering the ministry. It is this: *everyone* should be aware of all the issues involved in military service, including the pacifist position; he should study them carefully from every point of view; and then he should take his own position. No man can tell another man what that position should be; he can speak only for himself. But every man has an obligation to give consideration to all sides of the question.

The Man Undecided About His Own Faith

Can the man who has doubts about his own faith find those doubts resolved in seminary? There is no clear answer possible to this question, for the evidence is conflicting. Some men are helped; some men are not.

On the one hand some men clearly do have many of their questions resolved in seminary. They find themselves in a community that supports them as it encourages them to express their doubts while searching for their faith. One seminary student who had been asked to prepare a sermon on "My Faith" reported to his professor that he had so many doubts that he could not do this. Whereupon the teacher asked him to preach on "My Doubts." This exercise was the turning point in his own clarification of his faith. Such support may enable men to resolve their doubts and go forward to decide for the ministry.

On the other hand, some men with doubts believe that the seminary community as a whole is already so committed to the truth of the Christian religion that their questions are always prejudged and that they are not given the freedom they believe they need to work out their own position. They find themselves surrounded with men who for the most part have already made their decision and who, therefore, unconsciously exercise a coercive influence upon them. It may be that seminary hinders rather than helps them to come to their own free decision. In that case it is better for them to leave. This is far preferable to the tragedy of finishing seminary and going into the ministry with doubts still unresolved. This inner tension inevitably leads to a break in some form in later years.

The sum of the matter seems to be this: when in doubt, get the very best *and* most varied counsel you can. Do not go to *or* stay out of seminary on the advice of any one person. Once you have received as much wisdom as others can give you, then make up your own mind to the best of your ability, and act upon it. A rule-of-thumb principle that may be of help is: when in doubt, don't.

It is well to remind ourselves again that what is important is a man's relationship to God, and his response to it, with honesty and integrity. Whether he goes to seminary or not at this moment is not the crucial issue. What is crucial is God and his relationship to him.

In her book *The Parson Takes a Wife,* Maria Sheerin quotes a letter from her husband that applies here. He is discussing a call he had just received to go to another parish: "Instead of a clearly spoken 'Go' or 'Stay,' the Lord seems to say that He did not care whether calls were accepted or rejected, but He did care that the work, wherever it might be, was done in the name of the Lord, and not for the glorification of Charles Sheerin." [6]

[6] Maria Sheerin, *The Parson Takes a Wife* (The Macmillan Company, 1949), p. 131.

It is not very important at this point whether you go to seminary or not. What is important, however, is whether you finally do go—or do not go—for your sake or for God's sake.

The whole purpose of preparing for the possibility of the ministry by entering fully into life is to help you one day make your decision—whatever it may be—for God's sake.

6

How a Minister Is Educated

A divinity school is more than a place for the study of mysteries; it is a mystery in itself. Only those who have passed through the valley of the shadow of those years can fully know the special exaltations, the unique humiliations of becoming disciplined in theology. Coming in the hope of learning about God, the student is met abruptly with the fact of human ignorance: errors in scripture, doubts in theology, corruptions in the history of the institution, failures in the ministry to persons. In three years he must fit himself to save the world, a miracle that better men have not accomplished in two millennia. And yet—in a moment all this can be changed. In a class, hearing a phrase in the Greek that Paul spoke. In the chapel, hearing the tired voice of a teacher reading an ancient collect. In the kitchen over coffee, exchanging schemes for the rapid conversion of parishes. In the library, reading an assigned book. And so, in a moment unplanned and unexpected, despair becomes assurance, and the absurd, incredible notion that God can be known, and being known, served, becomes the only truth of any worth. In a community always anxious for a little thunder on the left, where even a small miracle now and then would do, he learns that the ordinary world is of extraordinary importance, and that piety can have the strength of intellect and be cleansed by the courage to test all things, holding fast that which is good.[1]

[1] *Forward Day by Day* (Advent 1960), p. 95.

THE PURPOSE OF THEOLOGICAL EDUCATION IS TO HELP MEN
and women grow in the knowledge and love of God and man.
It is carried on within a community made up of students and
teachers who live, study, and worship together. It is in their
meeting of one another and of God that theological education
takes place.

It is, therefore, an intensely personal experience. It has to do
with a man's growth in understanding God, man, and the Christian faith, and involves not simply the intellect but the whole
self. A man becomes educated theologically in part by the exercise of his intellect; in part by his commitment to God and his
fellowmen; and in part by his participation in the enterprise to
which he belongs—in this case the seminary community. Theological education begins long before he comes to seminary, and
continues until the day he dies, but in most cases this intensive
three-year formal education is the critical and most important
period.

Why Go to Seminary?
The Mystery of Motivation

Let some who are already in seminary speak for themselves.
A contemporary describes his experience this way. "I twisted
and dodged and turned and ran and hid. Now I give up. Obviously I can't ever live with myself again if I don't face it.
That's why I'm here in seminary."

Another student who had gone through very much the same
experience was greeted by an elderly woman who said to him:
"My, isn't that nice. How happy you must be now that you've
decided to be a minister."

The man replied: "Lady, I don't think it's very nice. God

knows I'm not happy about it. But there's nothing I can do about it at this stage."

For other men, on the contrary, the decision to enter the ministry seems simply the natural and normal one to make. One boy says, "The life of the church has always meant so much to me that I cannot recall a time when I did not want to be a clergyman."

Another comments: "All my life long I have known that I have been my best self when I have tried to follow what I believe Christ wanted me to do and when I could sit alone in church. There was something about the mystery of that building that drew me. I somehow knew that somebody was there —or something—so I tried to keep the spirit I found there when I went outside and mixed with people. For me not to go into the ministry would be the most awful tragedy that could occur."

The same kind of statement is made by another student: "If I should drop out of seminary, I would be dropping out of life. I just don't know where I'd go, for I know now there is no life if it is not the life of a minister."

Another one who finally made the decision to enter the ministry described it in this way. "As I look back at my life I do not see that it has been marked by any great or dramatic decisions. There have just been the normal amount of minor and, what seemed to me at the time, perhaps pointless little decisions, but they all added up and I found that I had come to a crossroads. Then I had to make what clearly was a big decision to go to seminary. But by the time I got to that crossroad it was unthinkable that I would have been content with any other decision."

One thing that can be said about men coming to seminary is that there is a mystery about it. There is a mystery about the call and man's response to it because there is a mystery about

God and the way God deals with man. Consider the mixed motivations that men have in coming to seminary:

Some are there to please their mothers; others to displease
their fathers.

Some come to seminary because they are afraid of independence; others because the only way they could establish their independence is to come.

Some are there because of a deep sense of sin; others because
of some vision of holiness.

Some come with humility, some with pride; and most with a
mixture of both.

Some men come because they are idealists and hope to make
the world a better place; others because they are afraid of the
world and seek the church as a refuge.

Some come because they have been a success in the world;
others because they have been failures.

Some come because they are drawn by the high demands that
are laid upon a minister's life; others because they will settle
for the security of the ministry.

Who can tell what it is that causes a man to go to seminary
and then into the ministry? God alone can tell. And that is
the whole point of the Christian life—that we are willing to
walk by faith. Apparently God calls men in this curiously mixed
fashion. Paul described the mystery in these words:

> By honour and dishonour, by evil report and good report: as
> deceivers, and yet true; As unknown, and yet well known; as
> dying, and, behold, we live; as chastened, and not killed; As
> sorrowful, yet alway rejoicing; as poor, yet making many
> rich; as having nothing, and yet possessing all things.[2]

As you go to seminary, then, you will find your fellow students coming from an infinite variety of backgrounds, struggling
with exactly the same questions. In the corporate life of the

[2] II Corinthians 6:8–10.

seminary, theological education takes place so that by the time you are ready to leave you are prepared to answer the question of the ministry for yourself because you have come to a deeper understanding of the mystery of both God and man.

The Seminary Community

The people who make up a seminary community are the students and the teachers. The latter will know more than the students about certain disciplines of theological education, but that knowledge does not mean that they necessarily know any more about God. *That* knowledge comes to them, as it does to every man, through repentance, humility, forgiveness, love, trust, and grace. It comes through meeting one another, accepting, understanding, judging, loving one another. In seminary, however, this is done through the particular relationship of a student with a teacher; the process by which they meet is the learning process; and the subject matter is provided by the theological disciplines.

The authors of the most significant study of theological education since the Second World War put it this way:

A theological school, like a church, is a community of Christian living and worship, but the axis on which the school turns is the relationship of teaching and learning. The elements in the encounter of teacher and student in theological study are for the most part those found in all educational endeavors. Subject matter has to be mastered; the student should discover his powers and limitations; and, as in all professional education, his knowledge and skills must be developed to make him adequate for the tasks he will face. But theological study has a dimension requiring special educational methods, yet transcending all method since it touches the realm of grace. Growth in Christian self-understanding and commitment cannot be bound to the formal categories of teaching and learning. The work of reading, classroom discussion, and lecturing must go on, yet the ultimate presupposition of all theological learning is that God's initiative and redemptive power are the ultimate resource.[3]

To what extent that "realm of grace" is a living reality in the seminary will be determined in large measure by the degree to which the teachers already have been possessed by that spirit. The quality of that spirit possessed by the teachers individually and in the *esprit de corps* of their faculty life is of critical importance for the students and for the quality of theological education that takes place.

The criteria that determine the worth of a seminary professor are the obvious ones: what he is as a scholar-teacher and what he is as a Christian person. His competency in his field should be beyond dispute; his own background should reveal solid preparation; and he should maintain some growing edge as a scholar so that he continues to make some contributions to the learned society of his professional colleagues and peers. The men who contribute most to theological education, as to any kind of education, are those who hold in some balance their responsibilities to both scholarship and teaching. It is expected that they possess the normal attributes of character of any Christian adult and also that they have a concern for what it is to be a seminary student and that they be ready to bring whatever they can of Christian faith from the experiences of their life to that of the students.

There is a mystery about the total life in the seminary community that is baffling to many entering students (as well as to many graduating students, professors and deans).

On the surface it appears to be just like the college community that you left a year ago or ten years ago, or just like any

[3] H. R. Niebuhr, D. D. Williams, and J. M. Gustafson, *The Advancement of Theological Education* (Harper, 1957), p. 112.

law school or medical school. To be sure there are daily chapel services usually, but these seem to be the only distinguishing marks that set it off from any other academic community. There are the same kinds of professors you have met before, some of whom seem more concerned about the minutiae of textual criticism than, let us say, the grandeur of God. You are told that you are preparing for the ministry in the twentieth century, and yet you are asked to spend hours studying a dead language. The day you arrived an upper classman carried your suitcases to your room, but three months later he walks by you in the hall as though he had never seen you before. You read about the quality of life of the early Christians—"See how they love one another"—but you see little evidence of that in your seminary. You want to reflect about God and the meaning of life, but the assignments are such that you have no time for such apparent luxuries.

The faculty are your teachers and somehow also your pastors. At the end of every semester they judge you and your work. How is it possible, you ask, for them to love me when they also judge me?

As you sense the response of your classmates to the seminary community the mystery deepens. For some of them coming to seminary is like coming home. For others seminary is a trial. One man will say, "When I stepped onto this campus I came alive all over," and his roommate will reply, "I came searching for something, and I find nothing."

There may be a partial explanation that helps illumine the mystery. A man comes to seminary, for example, with certain preconceived ideas of what a Christian community is. These ideas reflect, almost always, an inadequate theology; that is, a superficial or false understanding of God and the way he deals with men. It is only gradually that the average college graduate comes to understand that morality and Christianity are not identical; that there are an infinite variety of ways by which God deals with men; and the way he has dealt with that particular man may not be the way he deals with other men. It takes a long time to learn how to become open to other people; to discern in them the ways of God that are not ways you are familiar with; and to appropriate the spirit of mutual forbearance and acceptance of a common task to be done. Yet this is the way by which the seminary community is rebuilt year after year.

Theological education takes place in that mysterious and yet characteristic way by which God deals with men. It rests upon patience, understanding, and prayer. It means a willingness to be exposed to the best in education and to have the highest demands laid upon you in order that God may be revealed. God is the teacher, finally, and God somehow always breaks through to those men whom he is calling to his ministry.

When a seminary community is about its business—that is theological education—it is about God's business. Then in his hidden, interior fashion, in his good time, God breaks through all the human structures to confront the student face to face. It is in that community in that place that God has dealings with those whom he calls, and that place becomes for those men forever after a holy place.

This quality in the life of a seminary community comes with patience, quietness, and fidelity to the task at hand—helping men grow in the knowledge of both God and man. It is a mystery of grace and it is always a gift from God.

The Purpose of Theological Education

The Dean of the Harvard Medical School once had this to say about medical education:

. . . let me focus on two words, *education* and *training*. The best synonym for education is growth. No man can grow for another—no teacher can educate a student. Which is not to say that he cannot foster the student's learning, for that is precisely the contribution of a good teacher.

Training, on the other hand, is something that one can do to seals and dogs, and—unfortunately—to medical students and college students. Training is primarily the acquisition of factual knowledge and of techniques, while education seeks to stimulate the native curiosity of the learner, to help him see that a question can be asked, to ask it in such a way that data can be secured *pro* or *con* and then analyzed, leading to the formulation of a more penetrating question. Call this the "scientific method" if you wish. However that may be, it is the very heart of the learning process.

In talking about medical education, I have tried to emphasize that medical education is good only when it is good education. Thus, it is preferable to send medical students into the professional world knowing less, but understanding better how to learn. In any case, their stock of facts will become a steadily diminishing asset. If they have not learned while in medical school how to learn, they never will. And to be a good physician today requires that learning continue for life.[4]

One need only substitute the words *theological* for *medical* and *minister* for *physician* to understand the emphasis that will be made here: ". . . theological education is *good* only when it is good *education*. Thus, it is preferable to send theological students into the . . . world knowing less, but understanding better how to learn. . . . If they have not learned while in theological school how to learn, they never will. And to be a good minister today requires that learning continue for life."

The whole of theological education is a three-sided experience, for at its best a seminary is a learning community, a living community, and a worshiping community. All sides are related to one another; all are of equal importance; and if one side is lost then theological education is crippled.

[4] An address, "Medicine and Education," delivered by George Packer Berry on the occasion of the inauguration of Dr. Calvin Plimpton as President of Amherst College, reported in the *Amherst Alumni News*, Winter, 1961.

It might be put this way: the purpose of theological education is to cultivate the love of learning, the love of people and the love of God. Although these three are bound together in one unit, let us, for the sake of clarity, look at each in turn.

1. The Love of Learning

To begin with, the love of learning is to remind ourselves that we are called to love God with all our *mind*. When Jesus was asked what was the great commandment, he replied: "Thou shalt love the Lord thy God with all thy heart, and with all thy soul, *and with all thy mind*." [5]

Clearly the love of God involves more than intellectual love, just as love of one's neighbor is more than intellectual love. Yet this distinctive love "is required and possible since man is also mind and does not wholly love his loves if his mind does not move toward them. He cannot truly love with heart, soul and strength unless mind accompanies and penetrates these other activities as they in turn accompany and penetrate it." [6]

The core curriculum of a seminary is Biblical, historical, and theological. The Christian faith is a historic faith, arising from a historic event under the guidance of the God who is in control of all history and all peoples. The study of that faith and the continuing revelation of God to his people is a historic study. Since there has been a historic revelation of God it is important that what this has been in the past be studied in order that his ways in the present may be discerned.

There is another word to be said about the nature of theological study. Theological learning can take place only within the framework of faith. God is known only by those who trust

[5] Matthew 22:37.
[6] H. R. Niebuhr, *The Purpose of the Church and Its Ministry*, (Harper, 1957), p. 111.

him. It is necessary first to believe that he is, and then to commit oneself to him in order to have him reveal himself. This kind of knowledge is not unlike the knowledge of a person that is given, for instance, in friendship. You know a person, know what he really is, only as you believe in him and give yourself to him in trust; then he reveals himself. If you do not trust him, but only stand outside him, evaluating him, "sizing him up," he will not reveal himself to you and you will never come to know him.

It is complicated for the theological student, even beyond this, however, because the God whom he trusts is also the God whom he must study. He is called to commit himself into the hands of God and at the same time he is called to examine that God and the works of those hands. God is, in other words, both subject and object; he is both a living person to be trusted and an object to be studied.

This is a difficult task for any person to be given, yet it stands close to the heart of theological education. A student must carry on his studies and evaluate the object of his studies, else he is not truly a *student*. He must also carry them on within a relationship of trust and commitment to God, else he is not a *theological* student. This means personal involvement, and as Dr. Niebuhr comments: "If students are not personally involved in the study of theology they are not yet studying theology at all but some auxiliary science such as the history of ideas or ancient documents." [7]

There is a corollary to this. As the student learns about God he inevitably changes his concepts about him. This means— because of the personal involvement—that he is forced to change his concepts about himself. His ideas of God change, and changing ideas about himself invariably follow. As his thoughts about who God is become different, so do his thoughts about who he is. This can be an extremely painful experience. As one said:

[7] H. R. Niebuhr, *The Purpose of the Church* . . . p. 118.

"It is not simply that you find that the theology you came with was sentimental and inadequate; you discover that you take for your own the ideas of every theologian that you study in turn; then one day you find they all collapse and you are left without any theology at all. What do you do then?"

The answer of course is, "You hang on." You hang on until you learn the painful lesson that you cannot put your trust in any theology at all. You have to put your trust in God alone. If you will do that—even in those dark days when you are not at all sure even that he exists—then he will come in some fashion to you one day and you will be given some personal, firsthand knowledge of him. After that, you can begin to build your own theology. As it centers on Christ it will be Christian theology, and as it is enriched by the ideas of other theologians it will be an informed theology. But most important of all—as you build it *you* will become educated theologically yourself. So the answer is, "Hang on; this is why you have come to seminary." Of course you will change as your ideas of God change, but this is part of the purpose of theological education. "Theological education can be a refiner's fire, and no dross is consumed without changing the character of the metal." [8]

To be perfectly accurate in reporting about this intellectual side of seminary life, it must be said that some students do not find such academic experiences shattering, but rather emanicipating. They have often been secretly fearful that if they were to be Christian ministers they could not really be free to subject everything to critical intellectual inquiry. To discover, therefore, that part of theological education is directed specifically to digging out the facts, getting the record straight, asking "What is the truth of the matter?" is for these students an introduction into an exciting world of freedom where the only loyalty required is loyalty to truth. They are strengthened rather than shattered.

[8] H. R. Niebuhr, D. D. Williams, and J. M. Gustafson, *op. cit.*, p. 164.

The heart of the matter thus has to do with truth. Theological education should enable ministers to point beyond themselves to him who said, "I am the truth," without being afraid of any truth, no matter what its source. Perhaps more than any other factor this would help the church become a force in the intellectual life of society. This is part of its mission: to encourage all men to seek and respond to truth wherever they find it, confident that they are dealing (though they may not recognize it) with him who is the source of all truth and who sent his Son to reveal the truth about himself and all men.

What, then, is the material with which the student has to deal intellectually? The courses he will take in seminary will vary in accordance with his preparation and the requirements of his church and of the particular seminary he attends. In most instances, however, he will be required to take ninety points over a three-year period among the following fields: Biblical, Historical, Theological, and Practical. These fields in turn are usually divided as follows:

Biblical: Old and New Testament, Greek, Hebrew and other language study.

Historical: Church history, History of Religions or Comparative Religions.

Theological: Philosophy of Religion, Christian Doctrine or Systematic Theology, Christian Ethics.

Practical (or Pastoral): The Christian Ministry, The Church and The World, or the Mission of the Church, Religious Education, Psychology and Religion, Worship and Liturgics, Homiletics, Christianity and the Arts.

Courses that a student might expect to take during his first (Junior) year would typically be as follows:

First Semester

Old Testament: The history, literature and religion of Ancient Israel.

Systematic Theology: Introduction to Christian Theology.

Philosophy of Religion: An introduction to the main currents of Western philosophy.
Practical Theology: Introduction to Christian ministry.
One elective.

Second Semester
Old Testament: (continued)
New Testament: An introduction to the history, literature and religion of the New Testament.
Systematic Theology: (continued)
Practical Theology: (continued)
One elective.

In his second (Middler) year a student might be expected to include in his program:

Church History: The history of Christianity through the Reformation.
Christian Ethics: The foundation of Christian ethics.
Religious Education: The educational ministry of the Church.[9]

The remainder of his course of study would vary according to his individual interests and the divisional requirements for each field. There would be no great difference between this program in general and that in other seminaries, except in some, Church History would be given in the first year and theology in the second, and also in some seminaries at least a year of Greek would be required.

2. The Love of People

Theological education takes place within a community of people who are related to one another and to God. The knowledge of God that comes to those people will in part come to them through their human relationships. It might almost be said that the real purpose of a seminary is to create a living

[9] These course descriptions are taken from courses offered for students at the Union Theological Seminary, New York City, 1961–1962.

community, the members of which are bound together in theological study and worship, so that the living God might be known.

This emphasis upon human relationships is to serve as a reminder also that the Gospel is for people, that it is impossible to separate love of God from love of neighbor, and that the ministry means the service of man no less than the service of God. It has been placed squarely before us in the New Testament: "If a man say, I love God, and hateth his brother, he is a liar: for he that loveth not his brother whom he hath seen, how can he love God whom he hath not seen? And this commandment have we from him, That he who loveth God love his brother also." [10]

The seminary community is made up of men and women who are not simply learning together, but are living together. How they live, how they are concerned for and love one another has an important bearing upon how they are educated theologically. If they say that they love God but hate each other they are liars.

The community, without being irresponsible to the needs of the student, must give him all the freedom he needs to come fully to himself under God. The student must be helped to know that the seminary is concerned about him, and he must at the same time be protected from coercion from the community. When there is doubt as to which is called for in any instance, it is always better for the community to stand for freedom and let the student find his own way than to insist on responsibility and interfere with the free movement of the man's own spirit. This is a more difficult, indeed dangerous, position to take, for the student may not be capable at times of freely making the right decisions about himself, but it is the only way in which education can take place. The alternative is "training" a student, and that bears no resemblance to the education a

[10] I John 4:20–21.

student must receive if he is to develop his own resources under God.

Academic learning is never by itself sufficient to communicate the love of God. That love can be communicated only by loving people. The Gospel is not understood simply by the mind of man, but, given intellectual understanding, as it is transformed within the heart so that it is expressed in reasonable service and in common, human terms.

The development of those common, human terms is part of the responsibility of theological education. This means to help develop an outgoing concern for people—not simply seminary people or church people or good people, but all kinds of people.

There are usually three ways by which this is undertaken, although any particular seminary may stress only one or two of them. In general, however, this effort to develop the ability to relate personally to people is carried on through course studies, clinical training programs, and fieldwork assignments.

Just as there is a core curriculum around which the classical theological disciplines have been developed, so have there arisen certain fundamental areas within the modern disciplines. The primary ones are in psychiatry and psychology and in educational philosophy, methodology, and content. Descriptions of some typical courses may be sufficient to indicate these areas:

Religion and human development: The development of the individual through the life span from infancy to old age, with special attention to religious development and the factors in the life of the individual which influence and are influenced by that development.

Psychology and the pastoral office: A seminar on the work of the minister or religious worker as viewed in the light of his vocation and the roles which are expected of him. The focus of this course will be on the person and the functioning of the minister or religious worker as he fulfills his duties in the midst of the congregation or group. It is assumed that the student has already examined his normative roles; the explication of the total pastoral office will not be attempted. Rather, this course is an effort to further clarify the counseling opportunities of these roles in action. It is also an effort to build in the student the necessary critical habits for the continuing assessment of his vocation and role in counseling. Each student will be required to submit evaluative accounts of his own work with individuals or groups. Designed for seniors and graduate students.

The Church in contemporary society: The interaction of religion and society as revealed in the analysis of social structures which impinge upon the life and work of the church. An introduction to the sociology of religion with special attention to: mass culture and mass media, population problems, class stratification, and the social context of the church in urban and suburban cultures.

Religion in higher education: Highlights of the history and philosophy of higher education in Western culture, with special attention to religious perspectives and implications. Current analyses and critiques of "the university question." The role of the church and the Christian scholar in colleges and universities.

Christian education for adults: The significance of adult education in working out an educational strategy for the parish church. Consequent emphasis upon developing the theological study of the laity, occupational study groups, church officer training, parent education and appropriate forms of parish "social action." The relevance of the modern adult education movement for Protestant church education.[11]

The clinical training program normally takes place during twelve weeks in the summer, under the auspices of either the Council for Clinical Training [12] or the Institute of Pastoral Care.[13] These organizations direct programs, carried on under the supervision of accredited directors, in clinical settings, usually in general or mental hospitals or in penal institutions. There stu-

[11] These course descriptions are taken from the catalogue of the Union Theological Seminary, New York City, 1961–1962.
[12] Council for Clinical Training, 475 Riverside Drive, New York 27, New York.
[13] Institute of Pastoral Care, Box 57, Worcester 1, Massachusetts.

dents are given an opportunity to participate on the staff under the supervision of the chaplain, to observe the work of the institution itself in the care and rehabilitation of people, and to see in practice how some of the modern insights of such disciplines as psychology, psychiatry, and social work may be brought to bear to help in the total healing ministry. Clinical training is devised to acquaint them with a tool for the ministry so that they may better understand those to whom they are to minister and in the process come to a better understanding of themselves.

The fieldwork program that is undertaken by some seminaries is the third way by which students are helped to relate the Gospel (and themselves) to the life situations of people. At its best, this type of program calls for eight or ten hours of work a week by a student in a neighboring parish or institution. There, under the supervision of a minister or professionally trained worker, students are given an opportunity to work with people in a variety of activities that go on within the parish organization.

There is one further area that deserves mention as we consider ways by which students are helped to cultivate a love of people—the area immediately surrounding the seminary. If the seminary is in a rural area students frequently are given weekend assignments to assist in churches, sometimes with particular responsibility for young people's work. In cities the seminary itself sometimes has charge of a church, and the ministry is shared by professors and students; or a number of students may be made available on a regular basis to assist in storefront churches, both in the services and in the group activities.

No structure, of course, either an official one within the seminary or an informal one outside, can ever capture the art of living and loving people. That is caught, not taught. It comes in seminary through the mystery of Christian friendships. Like all such mysteries, these can never be structured. They simply appear, and one fine day you discover you have a friend. And the only difference from other friends is that he is a friend in Christ.

Part of this comes from the common life lived together, the same assignments shared, the same idiosyncrasies of professors to put up with, the same bafflement over the emotional involvement some students have over apparently minor issues (like candles in churches and the proper clerical clothing on clergymen), the same abysmal ignorance in areas where others display majestic learning. It is hammered out in joint tutoring sessions late at night when each man brings his specialty (will it be Greek, or the Thomistic arguments for the existence of God, or apocalyptic literature?) and puts it into the common pool of ignorance. It springs into being on the touch-football field or the baseball diamond or basketball court. It comes on subway rides to fieldwork assignments or late Sunday evenings over cups of coffee when weary students amuse each other by reciting the frustrating experiences of the day, including the sermons they heard that morning. However such friendships come, they come. And they are the substance of what it is to live and to love.

For some this gift of friendship comes in watching with a neighbor over his sick child in the hospital; baby-sitting for others when a parent dies; taking turns caring for all two-year-olds so some mothers may have a two-hour break once a week; comparing budgets and wondering how the ends are ever going to meet. Shared suffering, as do shared joys, brings the bond of friendship, particularly when such suffering takes men to the edge of their faith.

In other words, the learning of the love of people comes through the very fabric of life itself. Christian love comes where two or three are gathered together in the name of Christ. This is the point of Christian friendship—that men are gathered together, not around themselves, but because of another name and another loyalty. Christian friends always know that for the other, as for themselves, they are not their own, but belong to him in whose name they intend to minister. This brings a depth and a bond like that of no other friendship.

It may be the most enduring quality of seminary life, for many of these friendships stay with a man throughout his ministry. One of the greatest gifts that a seminary provides is this mystery of friendship in Christ. If this spirit can be made a normal and natural part of their theological education, then they will be able to bring the essential quality of the spirit of Christ in their ministry to people. They will have been able to learn the joy of loving people, and this is to learn to love life.

3. The Love of God

We turn now to the third and final principle upon which theological education is founded: the love of God. There is, we may remind ourselves, no such thing as the love of God apart from the love of learning (or truth) and the love of people, just as there can be no complete love either of truth or of man except those loves be undergirded by the love of God. These three principles are bound together in one whole.

At the same time there is a special emphasis that can be given to this third principle, for it is God finally who is responsible for men coming into the ministry, and it is to carry out his purpose that the ministry exists. All theological education —whether it be learning to study or to love people—is directed toward God. And theological education that omits this fact becomes nothing more than another graduate school.

Hence the importance of worship in a seminary. It has been put this way by Dr. Niebuhr: ". . . While a community which centers in worship is not a theological school, a theological school in which worship is not a part of the daily and weekly rhythm of activity cannot remain a center of intellectual activity directed toward God." [14]

This act of worship is related to and yet different from all the other acts that take place in a seminary. Or, to put it in another way, the act of worship takes all the other acts of study and living together and offers them to God.

> [Worship] is for students and faculty in general the most important alternation from study; in the context of praise and adoration the objects of theological study are set again in the context of churchly devotion. Diversity of points of view on questions of theology and church strategy is set in its proper light. The anxieties and guilt of students in the throes of becoming Christians are relieved in their renewed certainty of the faithfulness of God. For some students the life of worship and devotion brings the maturation process to its culmination; in worship they come to themselves. [15]

Worship, then, is an integral part of theological education. The regular gathering of the seminary community before God to praise him, to confess their sins before him, to pray to him is part of the ordered life the community can give a man as he begins to find his own way under God. As members of that community are truly responsible for one another and offer one another to God through their regular worship of him, they will support one another in a way that is not otherwise possible; and it may mark, as in no other way, the measure of the grace of God in that community.

Although the corporate worship of God is an end in itself, it clearly does have a strengthening influence upon the individuals in a seminary and upon their own personal life of prayer. God's love for each man and his answering, many times faltering, response of love in obedience to him is an intensely personal matter. There is always at bottom in each man this inner

[14] H. R. Niebuhr, *The Purpose of the Church* . . . pp. 129–131.
[15] H. R. Niebuhr, D. D. Williams, and J. M. Gustafson, *op. cit.*, p. 190.

conversation—the interior life in what William James called "the dumb region of the heart"—between him and his God. It can never be shared with another human being, for it is conversation only with the One with whom he has final dealings. This inner life is thinking and brooding and praying. It revolves around the ways God deals with man in general but in particular with each man; and in time the center of his existence comes to be in this inner sense of living before and with God. It is the *only* way to firsthand personal knowledge of God.

Carlyle was once asked what kind of man they were looking for as minister in his church, and he replied, "We are looking for a man who knows God—and not by hearsay." In this inner personal relationship with God where a man brings all his experiences—the high and the low, the noble and the mean, the victories and the failures, his choices and refusals—and lays them before God and waits upon him, this firsthand knowledge is gradually given.

In that life, within which no other ever sees, he confesses to God his inmost sins, he thanks him for his gifts, he asks him for his help, he offers his concern, and the world's, to him. And underneath it all there will be growing a desire finally to love God, or at least to want to love him. So along with his prayers that he says in his heart there comes a gradual turning of his will, his being, to God. He finds that he is more and more sustained by an undercurrent toward God. There is, then, an inner power—a sense of freedom under God—that begins to carry him and is increasingly the source of his strength. He is *personally* related to God, and in that relationship finds all he needs for the task at hand—now in the seminary as a student and later in the world as a minister.

Theological education, then, means the education of the whole man. The whole man is one who has learned how to relate his learning and his living to God. He has come to realize that his study is worship, as his love is worship, and that complete worship is no less than his whole study and life offered to God. Insofar as he is given some understanding of what these three-fold loves mean in relation to one another he not only has begun his theological education but also sees that it is to continue throughout his ministry and ends only when he makes his final offering to God at the completion of his life.

The Personal Equation

Enough has now been said about theological education to make it clear that what is important is not so much what one learns as what one becomes. In seminary the real question is: What happens to *you?* Your learning is significant as it does something to you, and your theology is important as it is lived. The Christian faith has a vitality as it is appropriated by you as a living faith.

The first key is the *acceptance of yourself.* Someone has said that Popeye and St. Paul both have the same philosophy of life: "I am what I am"; except that St. Paul adds, "by the grace of God." In either case the point is this: we do not have to fight against ourselves, be ashamed of ourselves, try to reform ourselves, or pretend that we are not as other men. We are what we are.

Acceptance of yourself is in turn a key to the *acceptance of others.* This means in seminary a willingness to be open to other men, other points of view, other understandings of God and different interpretations of nature, man, and the universe; in a word to be willing "to live and let live." This is not to deny the right to one's own conviction. It is simply to affirm that the way to theological understanding is more by affirming one's own belief of what is true than by denying the belief of others. Baron Friedrich von Hügel once wrote: "It is by my not denying as false what I do not yet see to be true, that I give myself the chance of growing in insight." [16] You take your place on the basis of your convictions; let others take theirs; give witness to your own understanding of the truth; but do not use your energy attacking the witness or the integrity of your brothers.

Along with the acceptance of yourself there is also the *affirmation of yourself*. You are not meant to be (or become) somebody else. You are meant to be yourself. To pretend to be somebody else is to be "two-faced"; it is to be a hypocrite.

One of the obstacles before many men before they go to seminary is their belief that to become a minister they must become somebody quite different from what they are. Nothing is further from the truth: you have to be yourself.

You are meant to be a whole person as you prepare for the ministry. You are to enter into life just as fully as you can, and you can best do this as you launch out into the mainstream of life and let yourself appear to be just what you in fact are. If there is any single human characteristic that people look for in their minister, it is that he "ring true" as a human being. You can prepare the way for this best in seminary by simply being and affirming yourself as you are.

There is a corollary to this. You are also called *to help others affirm themselves*. Our neighbors in seminary, as the people to whom we later shall minister, have the same responsibility: to be what they believe they are meant to be under God. They have to make that decision for themselves as we for ourselves. We cannot do it for them. What we can do, however, is to give them freedom to make their decision and then to support them in it. This is critically important when they have come to a decision that they believe is in accordance with the will of God for them and when we are in disagreement with that decision. Having expressed ourselves to them, our principle responsibil-

[16] *Essays and Addresses*, I, 14; quoted in H. Dakin, *Von Hügel and the Supernatural* (Society for the Promotion of Christian Knowledge, 1934), p. 14, n. 1.

ity is then to give them support and strength. Our Christian concern is always to affirm others in their existence as we try to affirm our own.

The reason that you can accept and affirm yourself of course is because *you are God's*. You begin to know that you are not wholly your own but that the whole point of your life is being yourself under God. Indeed, you gradually come to see that the effectiveness of your ministry rests precisely upon this awareness that it is God who is important and that you are somebody only because you are God's. The purpose of your ministry, you gradually come to realize, is to help your people understand that they are God's too. You know who they are because you know who God is—and that both they and you belong together and to him.

So the personal equation continues throughout a man's lifetime. In the long run the quality of his ministry is determined by the quality of his life. That began to be formed long before he entered seminary, but the direction it will take and its shaping will largely be decided by him during his three years of theological education.

The Choice of Seminary

Broadly speaking, there are two types of seminaries on the American scene: the interdenominational seminaries that are usually affiliated with, or a part of, a university, and the denominational seminaries that may be affiliated with a university but usually are independent.[17] Whether one chooses an interdenominational or denominational seminary depends upon many factors: educational, personal, and ecclesiastical.

---

[17] A list of the seminaries that belong to the American Association of Theological Schools may be obtained by writing to the Executive Director, 934 Third National Building, Dayton 2, Ohio.

The interdenominational seminaries are seminaries made up of many different denominational loyalties. If there is any church control it is always from a number of churches. Although they are founded to serve the church, their affiliation is more likely to be with a university. The faculty and student body alike are made up of members of various denominations, and usually represent a wide range of backgrounds and interests.

Because of the university setting, primary emphasis is given to the intellectual side of theological education. Academic standards are high and are important. The course offerings tend to be generous, and opportunity is given for students to take courses beyond the theological disciplines within the university. Generally provision is also made for graduate study, so that the seminary community has not only students preparing for the B.D. degree but for advanced degrees as well.

The marks of such a seminary community are usually freedom and stimulus. There is an excitement in the air where any theological position that one holds is challenged immediately by others. There is never any corporate constraint to accept any single theological position or to affirm any particular church loyalty. One is exposed to a vast variety of theological points of view, church traditions, and ways of worship. And a man is free to make his own way and to come to his own conclusions and convictions about where he stands. If he already belongs to a denomination, he will usually find that his loyalty to it is strengthened as he learns to value its emphasis in relation to others.

The denominational seminary, on the other hand, tends to stress what is held in common by members of that denomination. The framework within which a theology is worked out is always a commonly accepted framework (though that may be so wide in some instances that it is not a very restricting factor). There is always a common tradition of worship that is carried out (though again even within any single denomination there may be quite a variety of forms). Whatever the denomination, there is an awareness of and concern for the church, so that students are exposed naturally to a sense of the church's ministry and most frequently to its parochial or congregational expression.

The academic emphasis normally is directed more to meeting the standards expected by the church than by the university. Those denominational seminaries that are affiliated with a university tend to stress more the intellectual and academic demands in preparation for the ministry. There is usually a sense of a deeply knit community of men who know where they belong and what they are preparing for.

The precise question, "Which kind of seminary should I choose?" can of course be answered only in relation to a particular person. Certain general principles may be suggested, however, that follow from the above descriptions.

The student who has yet to make up his mind both about the Christian faith and his own place in the ministry probably will respond more positively to life in an interdenominational seminary. There he will find freedom; there is no particular pattern that is appropriate for him to follow; there will be many differing points of view presented; many of his contemporaries will be as undecided as he is. If he is a good student, so much the better. A student who is not yet ready to commit himself, who is still inwardly moving and has many doubts, will probably feel less under coercion at this kind of seminary.

By the same token the man who has substantially made up his mind about the Christian faith and his place in the ministry, who is ready to "dig" so that he gets his roots grounded in one tradition, will be ready for a denominational seminary. One who feels the need for the support of a more homogeneous community and in particular the familiar forms of worship also will probably feel more at home there.

These generalizations are, of course, too general to be of any significant use apart from personal counsel with the individual concerned. So do not take any principle as absolute. For what they may be worth, however, they are general observations that should then be adapted to your particular case with the assistance of a wise counselor.

Continuing Theological Education

The theological education that a man receives in seminary is neither the beginning nor the ending of his learning about God and man. It is merely the most intensive and formal period of theological education that he will have.

In a sense it can be said that his seminary education will have been a success if it makes clear to him the necessity to continue it, and gives him suggestions how to do it. The knowledge of God and man should continue on deeper and deeper levels the more a man lives and carries on his ministry. To keep his continuous living experience related to regular study and regular prayer is to continue his theological education. The elements are the same whether the education takes place in seminary or in the pastorate: learning—people—God. With regular time for study and with regular time for prayer, the experiences of the ministry will guarantee strength and vitality to his continuing education.

Another way of stating this is to say that a man's theological education is continued in the ministry on the basis of his experiences as a minister. So we can turn now to consider just what those experiences are that a man has once he leaves seminary and embarks upon the ministry.

7

The Minister: A Many-Sided Man

THERE ARE MANY SIDES TO THE MINISTRY, AND A MAN WHO becomes a minister soon discovers that he is called to be a many-sided man. He is to be all things to all men while remaining faithful to God alone.

Although his work has many sides, he has only one life. Gradually his work becomes his life and his life becomes his work. The many-sided man becomes an integrated, whole man because he is, he knows, always God's man. So he goes about his work and he goes about living: many sides to it, but one spirit.

He preaches sermons to the faithful and calls on the faithless. He is a friend of his people and a citizen of his community. He prays for the world and votes for his party. He administers sacraments and works a mimeograph machine. He reads books in his study and washes dishes in the parish house. He teaches little children and gives lectures to adults. He visits the sick and elderly and goes to the ball game with the young. He spends time in prison and calls policemen by name. He walks freely into social agencies and knows who owns the neighborhood bar. He prays at banquets of bankers and labor leaders, and asks God's blessing upon both. He is a companion of the wealthy as of the poor, and is owned by neither. If he is married, he is also a husband and may be a father—and his ministry is at home as it is abroad. In brief, he is a many-sided man.

What does a minister do? The most direct answer is that he does the work of Christ. He is commissioned to carry out the work of the office that was established by Christ. All ministers carry out the work he first called the original disciples to do. His ministry was in large measure devoted to instructing them in what their ministry was to be. He introduced them to some understanding of the mystery of who he was, who his father was, who they were, and who all men were. He taught them that they were to minister in accordance with his example and by the power that he would give them. They came to understand that as he, so they, were not to be ministered unto, but to minister, and that this meant service to God and to man.

Christ taught them that the work he had to do, was also theirs. He commissioned them to preach the Gospel to all nations, and he promised them the gift of the Holy Spirit. This Spirit was given them at Pentecost, and empowered them to carry out the work for which they had been commissioned.

At the outset, therefore, the work of the apostles and the work of the church was bound together. The authority given the apostles since then has been transferred by the church through the power of the Holy Spirit to men called to exercise the work of the ministry.

There have been changes in the development of the historical forms by which Christians have maintained that authority—through bishops, presbyters (or priests) together, local congregations, and through a combination of these—but there has never been any question about the essential nature of the work ministers have been commissioned to do: to preach the Gospel and to administer the sacraments.[1] There has been, then, for

---

[1] ". . . In the Catholic tradition the fullness of the Christian priesthood properly belongs to the episcopate, presbyters possessing a share in

every generation of ministers from the beginning in whatever Christian tradition both a call to the ministry and then authority to carry out the work of the ministry. As men have been ordained by the Holy Spirit through the church, they have been given authority to do the work to which they have been called.

The office of the ministry exists, therefore, in order that the mission of the church may be carried out. As we have seen, that mission is to those who live in the world outside the church. The task of the total ministry of the church—that is, lay people and clergy together—is to bring to all men the saving knowledge of life in Christ. It is the work of the minister to help the lay people of the church carry out their ministries where they work and live. There are five sides to this work: pastor, preacher, priest, teacher, and administrator. We shall look at each in turn.

1. The Minister as Pastor

The traditional meaning of the word *pastor* is *shepherd*. Jesus describes himself as the Good Shepherd in these words:

> I am the good shepherd: the good shepherd giveth his life for the sheep. . . .

it by delegation. However, in practice most priestly functions are commonly exercised by the presbyter, only certain special rights, including the crucial privilege of ordination, being reserved to the bishop. Such an order of priests is for the larger part of Christendom, today as in the past, central in the liturgical life and pastoral work of the Church." E. R. Hardy, Jr., "Priestly Ministeries in the Modern Church," in H. R. Niebuhr, D. D. Williams, and J. M. Gustafson, *The Advancement of Theological Education,* pp. 150 f.

The Presbyterian tradition maintains that the presbyter himself is a bishop and that the fullness of the Christian priesthood as well as the episcopacy, including "the crucial privilege of ordination" belongs to the presbyter. Perhaps the most central issue to be resolved in all attempts to unite the churches is the interpretation of the place and authority of the bishops.

I am the good shepherd, and know my sheep, and am known of mine.

As the Father knoweth me, even so know I the Father: and I lay down my life for the sheep.

And other sheep I have, which are not of this fold: them also I must bring, and they shall hear my voice; and there shall be one fold, and one shepherd.[2]

The minister is, in the words of George Herbert, "a father to his flock," who knows the individual members by name and has come among them to serve them. It is an intensely personal and intimate relationship in which minister and people are bound together. In one service of ordination the bishop reminds those who are about to be ordained of the character of that relationship with these words: "Have always therefore printed in your remembrance, how great a treasure is committed to your charge. For they are the sheep of Christ, which he bought with his death, and for whom he shed his blood. The Church and Congregation whom you must serve, is his Spouse, and his Body." [3]

The pastor is one who in himself and in his office represents Christ caring for his sheep. It has been said that as a teacher is concerned with the mind, and the physician with the body, so the minister is concerned with the soul. He must therefore be familiar with those deepest matters of the soul, understand the rules that have to do with the soul's health, and be able to apply them. He is to help men and women discern the ways of God in their lives, to give them some confident assurance that God is with them, to point out in love the truth about their lives that may be difficult for them to understand, and to assure them that he will stay with them no matter how difficult the going may be. It is for this reason that Baxter urged his fellow ministers, "I earnestly beseech you . . . for the sakes of your people's

[2] John 10:11 and 14–16.
[3] "The Form and Manner of Ordering Priests," *Book of Common Prayer*, p. 540.

souls, that you will not slightly slubber over this work . . . but make it your great and serious business." [4]

When a minister goes into a new parish his people will come to know him within a short period of time as he reveals himself through his preaching. He will know his people, however, only as he comes to them as a pastor. This means as he identifies himself with his people by coming to know them and by "calling them by name."

The pastoral ministry is carried out effectively on the basis of four principles.

a. GO WHERE THE PEOPLE ARE

You will not come to know your people until you go where they are. No matter how good a mousetrap you may build, people will not beat a path to your door until they first know that you are interested in them, their problems, and their lives. This they will understand as you go where they are.

Every minister who has been a pastor to his people has had the experience of a parishioner coming to him when he was in trouble, and saying: "I have a problem that I have to talk over with somebody. I'm calling on you because I remember you called on me." This means incorporating a regular schedule of calling on the members of one's congregation as part of the backbone of the pastoral ministry.

Part of the value of calling rests on the old adage, "A housegoing parson makes a churchgoing people," though there may be no virtue simply in going to church. It does however provide the best opportunity to know your people by name. You can know people only as you call on them, and they are most themselves in their homes.

[4] Richard Baxter, "The Reformed Pastor," quoted in S. W. Hudson, "The Ministry in the Puritan Age," in Niebuhr, *et al., op. cit.,* p. 193.

The most critical calls are those made upon the sick. When a person has been taken out of the normal routine of his life, has had his clothes and money taken from him, and has been placed in a hospital bed and told that there he must remain for some time, he is brought face to face with some of the fundamental issues of his life in a way that is not possible when he is busily involved in life. He has an opportunity to review where he has been and to rethink once again where he is going. Reflections of this kind are of tremendous religious significance. For a clergyman to come in regularly during these periods will enable a pastoral relationship to be established that will carry on for years afterward. Confidences are made, friendships developed, and faith often begun through such regular hospital calling.

Perhaps the wisest word of counsel to young clergymen in their first parishes was given by a minister who had served for many years in a hospital. "If your very first calls in a parish," he comments, "are made upon the people who are sick, it will establish you in the minds of all the people in that parish as one who cares. This is the heart of the pastoral ministry; so go see your sick people first."

b. LISTEN TO PEOPLE

The pastoral ministry is in large measure "the ministry of listening." A number of things happen when you are willing to listen to people. The first is that you find out where the problem lies, or at least where they think it lies. You find out what people have on their minds. They are given an opportunity to express their concerns, their problems, their difficulties, and hopes. It is only by listening that you can discover where the people inwardly are living.

Second, the very fact that you are willing to listen establishes a personal relationship. The hard fact of the matter is that in our contemporary culture there are not very many people who are willing to listen to other people. Doctors, psychiatrists, social workers, clergy—all people who are in the "helping professions"—know that a very large measure of therapy and healing comes simply by listening.

One clergyman who has concentrated in his ministry on listening describes an episode where a man came into his office and at first was unable to speak. The counselor simply sat waiting for the duration of the interview, making clear by his words and manner that he would be happy to wait until his visitor was ready to talk. At the end of an hour the visitor finally got up and thanked him, saying, "Next time when I return I will be able to talk." At the next visit the relationship was established because the minister had been willing to listen.

When people are hurt in life they want to tell somebody about it. The little boy who is hit on the head by a friend runs home to cry to his mother, "Tommy hit me." It is not the bruise to the head but the bruise to the ego that causes the pain. When bruises come in life, as they inevitably do, there is something deeply embedded in our nature that causes us to cry out to someone, "I got hit." That someone is a pastor.

Furthermore, it is only by listening that one can accurately identify the basic problem. The underlying problem is seldom the superficial problem, the one spoken about first. The individual who needs help may have a complete misunderstanding of the area where he needs the most help, and may be utterly confused as to where the real difficulty lies. It is only by listening that diagnosis is possible.

One man in his early fifties came to see his minister because he was having trouble with his wife. After he had talked for some time it was perfectly apparent that his trouble stemmed, not from difficulty in the marriage, but from a sense of frustration in business. He had failed to receive an expected promotion. It was now clear to him that he had reached the plateau in his company, and that he was not going to go all the way to the top. In his desire to hit back at life, and unable to hit back at an anonymous group decision made on a higher echelon, he turned against his wife. She was simply the nearest one upon whom he could vent his anger. He felt he could "get back at" life by expressing hostility at this level.

When he was able to identify the problem correctly, the domestic situation cleared up. He resigned his position and went into business for himself. Though his earnings were not so great, his sense of personal satisfaction and fulfillment more than compensated. He became a whole human being—and this meant becoming a good husband.

Listening also enables a minister to recognize when he is unable to be of significant help. When an individual is in need of specialized assistance, it is important for the pastor to make the proper referral to a better qualified source. It may be economic necessity, in which case reference can be made to the social-service organization. More likely it will be deep-seated emotional needs that require the services of a professional counselor. A minister should be trained adequately in interpersonal relationships so that he can discern the danger signals in a person's mental or emotional makeup that clearly call for professional assistance. He then can refer the person intelligently to a psychiatrist or other appropriate person.[5]

c. SPEAK

Christian ministers are not simply counselors whose primary function is to listen. Although there is a time for silence (a much

[5] Professional counseling is a very specialized, highly technical art, requiring training over and above that given men in the course of the usual B.D. program. There are some counseling programs offered for advanced work in a few of the seminaries associated with universities, which would qualify a minister to concentrate in a counseling ministry. Such positions, apart from associated responsibilities, such as a chaplain, are limited.

longer time than we should like to admit), there is also a time for speaking (usually much briefer).

If the minister has something to say he should say it. If not, he should keep silent. Any pastor, however, who is set in the midst of his people and has had opened to him the personal crises of their lives will find the word to speak when it is the season for speaking, for the eternal Word of God is given for times of crisis: to the fearful, the word of hope; to the sinner, the word of forgiveness; to the dying, the word of life; to the separated, the word of reconciliation. The heart of the pastoral ministry is in the speaking of the right word at the right time.

(*1*) *Affirmation* A minister is meant to speak with authority when he is concerned with the fundamental affirmations for the Christian faith. Since he knows what God has done in Christ for all men, he should speak with clarity in translating the great truths into personal truths that can be appropriated by individuals for their personal use.

When a minister is face to face with a parishioner who has just been told that he has a fatal illness, what is he to say? Can he make some affirmation that will ring true?

Exactly what he says and how he says it will depend upon that intuitive pastoral sense that is developed over the years, but there can be no question about the essential content of what he says: Christ has destroyed the power of sin and death. He is the Lord of life and of death. There are many rooms in his father's house, and he has gone to prepare a place for us that where he is we may be.

There need be no hesitation about affirming certain fundamental moral laws that exist in life. The "law of love" causes life to flourish, and disobedience to that law causes life to be destroyed. When a personal relationship has been broken, for example, the only way that it can be restored is by one of the persons involved saying, "I am sorry." So long as people refuse to confess that they are sorry, the relationship will continue to be broken. It is as simple (and as difficult) as that: it is a law.

(2) *Forgiveness* The essential meaning of the Gospel is that God loves us. "God so loved the world, that he gave his only begotten Son, that whosoever believeth in him should not perish, but have everlasting life." [6]

No matter therefore what we have done, how terrible our offense, one essential fact about us is that God loves us. This can be affirmed without any qualification. There is nothing—absolutely nothing—that can prevent us from making our peace with God. Indeed, it has been put as strongly as this: the only sin that God cannot do anything with is when we give up. We ought, therefore, never to give up, but to confess our sins to God, recognize that we are forgiven, and get on with the business of living.

The absolving power of the ministry is an essential part of the minister's office. The ministry has been given to set people free from their sins. Assurance of this forgiveness may come through the pastoral relationship, or in the sacramental ministry of confession, or through the preaching of the Word of God. However the word of forgiveness is heard, it is a word that is at the heart of the meaning of the Christian Gospel.

A young man may express best what this means when he says, upon leaving a minister's study, "Thank heaven, now I've gotten this off my chest I can begin again." Or it may be spoken by a woman who says, "I feel now as though a great burden had been lifted from my shoulders." In one way or another each has heard: "Go in peace. Thy sins have been forgiven thee."

(3) *Counsel* The pastor is to speak "the truth in love." [7] This means that he has to bring the best wisdom that his education and experience have afforded him to bear upon the problems of his people, and out of his concern for them to express what he understands the truth to be.

[6] John 3:16.
[7] Ephesians 4:15.

To consider the pastoral ministry as a supportive ministry only is to misinterpret the pastoral office. There will, of course, be times when the word spoken must be an overpowering word of comfort. The people of God are to be "comforted." Yet the Biblical meaning of the words, "to comfort" is "to strengthen." People cannot be strengthened if they are not helped to see the truth, and to respond to it. This may, of course, be painful at times, but in the long run it is the only way to health and genuine power for living.

From one point of view the counsel may be nothing more than common sense. The pastor is able to bring common sense because he has a different perspective, has had over the years a good deal of experience, and is not himself so involved as the one who comes to him for help.

Common sense, however important and helpful, provides only part of the counsel that can be offered. The heart of the pastoral relationship rests upon the ability of the pastor to help people see how God already is acting in their lives.

The purpose of all pastoral counseling, in other words, is to help people to come to know God. Typical questions are: "How can I see God when life is so terrible?" "Has God decided to punish me in this tragedy?" "Does God have anything to say to me?" "Why is it that God has let this happen?" The pastor is expected to have some answers to these questions.

A young couple about to be married are ready to hear what God has to say to them through the great experience of mutual human love. How can they be helped to see that they are "bearers of God to each other?" In their human love they catch a little glimpse of God's eternal love. They represent nothing less than the grace of God to each other. It is the pastor's task to help them realize this.

Parents do not own their children, to use another example. Try to own them, and you will lose them. Children are a gift from God. They are given to parents in order that they may come to know God. That knowledge will come as parents are willing to set them free from themselves and grow in their own understanding. How can parents be helped to see that the setting free of their children is the only way in which their children will come back to them finally?

The great mystery of suffering—particularly undeserved suffering—is perhaps the most critical area in the pastoral ministry. It is central to the meaning of the Gospel. The mysterious intermingling of creativity and suffering, of tragedy and hope, of pain and nobility provide the very stuff of life. A pastor is given a unique opportunity to help his people see that this stuff is the means whereby Christian life becomes a reality.

There are no superficial answers to the mystery of suffering. A pastor who has pat and ready answers is not trusted. Platitudes have no power. Easy explanations of the mystery turn people away from Christ rather than draw them to him. Sometimes all that is necessary is just to be with a person.

One evening a minister called on a woman member of his congregation who was in a hospital for an operation. He waited with her husband until she was brought down from the recovery room. Some weeks later the husband called on the minister and said to him: "I will never forget your call that night. When you walked into the hospital room I knew somehow that everything was going to be all right." The minister replied, "But you know, I didn't do anything," to which the man replied, "That is precisely the point. You didn't have to do anything. You were there. And it was you who were there."

When all is said and done, people will be helped not so much by the pastor's wise counsel as by the fact that he was utterly honest *and* that he stood with them in their time of need.

The way of the Cross is the way of life. This is true. It is not, however, a truth that is communicated by words spoken. It is a truth that can be known only as it is lived. This is what is known as "doing the truth." When one is willing to respond to life in this way, then the whole drama of the Christian religion begins to take on a vitality and a power that until then had eluded the person.

This is particularly true as one is led to grapple with the depths of the mystery of the suffering of Christ on the Cross. Emily Dickinson once wrote in a letter to a friend, "When Jesus tells us about his Father, we distrust him; when he shows us his home, we turn away, but when he confides to us that 'he is acquainted with grief' we listen, for that too is an acquaintance of ours." Just because our acquaintance is with the mystery of grief and suffering, we may be able to discern something of the meaning of the mystery of the Cross and how it is related to the mystery of the cross in our lives.

Theologically this means we see the key to the mystery in Christ, the Lamb of God slain before the foundation of the world, the one who expressed the mind of God on the Cross. It shows God's full power when there is obedience to love. In terms of Christian living, then, no suffering need be useless; out of weakness strength is given; the life of faith in response to love leads to a life with God and his power.

In a pastoral sense the point is that if ministers help people to see what God's action in Christ really means, then they may have faith that he is still with them in their present suffering, and so they can be strengthened to step into the future with confidence. They have been "comforted" because they have been "strengthened." It is the most satisfying work of the pastor.

There is one concluding word to be said about a pastor's speaking. Pastoral relationships are *absolutely* confidential. The only time a minister should speak about a pastoral relationship is when he has received permission from the person involved. Other than that, no word should ever escape his lips about the nature of that pastoral confidential relationship.

d. PRAY FOR PEOPLE

Undergirding every pastoral function is the prayer of the pastor for his people. What he is able to accomplish will be determined in large measure by the integrity of his intercessory prayer. Since "more things are wrought by prayer than this world knows of," it is important for him to offer to God his people, confident that God will do for them greater things than he can either hope or pray for.

As part of his normal pastoral ministry, he will regularly offer intercessions to God for his people in some ordered way. It may be as simple a division as on a geographic basis or according to names alphabetically or by birthdays. Any procedure is satisfactory as long as it is all-inclusive and is followed out regularly. "There is no greater intimacy with another than that which is built up through holding him up in prayer," Douglas Steere writes:

> The firm bond that existed between John Frederic Oberlin and his parish was laid each morning in the hour that he devoted to prayer for his individual parishioners. We are told that as they went past his house at this hour in the morning, they did so in quiet, for they knew what was happening there. Forbes Robinson's *Letters to His Friends* reveal his constant use of this form of prayer for his Cambridge associates. He remarks in one letter that if he would really reach some need in his friend's life, he would always prefer a half-hour's silent petition for him to an hour's conversation with him.[8]

God is the one who ministers as the relationship between him and his people is strengthened by the prayer of the pastor. So the place of God increases while the place of the pastor decreases. If the minister has been in the middle long enough to establish the relationship, then he has been an effective pastor.

[8] D. V. Steere, *Prayer and Worship* (Hazen Foundation, 1941), p. 31.

2. *The Minister as Preacher*

Preaching is telling the story of the Good News of the Gospel so that the people who hear it respond to God with a deeper knowledge and love of him. It is presenting Christ in the worship of the church so that those who gather together in his Spirit are strengthened by his presence. It is the proclamation of the living Word of God as by "a dying man to dying men."

It is relating the "old, old story of Jesus and his love" to people who live in the new nuclear age. It is the Holy Spirit speaking to the hearts of men and women through a minister who has placed himself under the Word that it may be presented to their condition. It is a drama acted out by God and his people with the minister serving (to use a figure of Kierkegaard's) as prompter. It is the power of God to correct the hearts of men of sin and to make them holy; it is to forgive and to strengthen.

Whatever the definition, the preaching office is always concerned to hold together people and the Gospel. It is the Word of God directed to the lives of people together with the response of people to God and to one another. Certain conditions follow.

The minister who is to preach with power must know the people who are in the pews. He will know them there because he knows them in their homes. If he is to be a preacher he must first be a pastor. All good preaching arises out of the lives of the people.

The immediate background of all preaching, therefore, is provided by the personal lives of the congregation. Indeed, in some measure good preaching is good personal counseling. Sometimes the very anonymity of a service of worship may enable a person to hear the word more easily than when it is spoken to him personally. Harry Emerson Fosdick, one of the great American preachers of the twentieth century writes these words in his autobiography: "I am commonly thought of as a preacher, but I should not put preaching central in my ministry. Personal counseling has been central. My preaching at its best has itself been personal counseling on a group scale." [9]

The preacher is concerned not simply with the personal lives of his parishioners but also with the society in which they live. It is, therefore, of crucial importance that he understand that society, that he study the forces that have brought it into being and those that are at work changing it. The Gospel in its essential message is an eternal Gospel that does not change. The world where that Gospel is heard, however, does change.

So the minister will be aware of the thought-forms that make it possible for men to believe in the twentieth century and those that make it very difficult for men to believe. It is, for example, a world where it is popularly believed that science has supplanted religion. Those disciplines that make up society, insofar as they are "scientific," infer that if God is not dead he is at least very unimportant. Ideas that arise out of the ferment of scientism, Marxism, existentialism, psychiatry, sociology, anthropology, naturalism, humanism, and nearly all other contemporary disciplines have as a basic presupposition the irrelevance of religious faith.

These ideas are in the backs of the minds of the people in the pews. They may not even know that they have them, but they are there because they are in our society and they are deeply embedded in the systems of education. These perfectly obvious facts have to be recognized and wrestled with if the Gospel is to have any significant bearing on life as it is lived today. One recent seminary graduate put it in these words: "We clergy know too little about the world in which our people live and too much about the world in which Jesus lived. And I am afraid we tend

[9] H. E. Fosdick, *The Living of These Days* (Harper, 1956), pp. 214–215.

to think that the world in which Jesus lived is much like the one in which our people are living."

The preacher has a responsibility to be faithful not only to his people by understanding their society but also to God by proclaiming his Gospel. That Gospel, as we have seen, is not an exhortation to men to act in a certain way; it is a declaration that God has already acted in his way. The Good News of the Gospel declares that God has forgiven sin, overcome death, and destroyed the power of evil. The forces ranged against him have done their worst, and he has overcome them in Christ.

Therefore man is to respond. Because God has acted in a certain way, it *therefore* follows that men are to act in a certain way. In other words, Christian ethics follow from the nature of God. The God who has revealed himself in the Judeo-Christian tradition is a God whose very nature is love. His will is the establishment of a world where love and justice prevail. All preaching must include the implication of the *therefore* ethics. To avoid them is to deny the nature of the Christian God.

The preacher to be faithful to this Gospel must, therefore, be a prophet. To be a prophet is to speak in behalf of God about the issues of society. It is to point out on behalf of God the meaning of all of the forces at work in the social structure. It is, for example, to point to the issue of segregation and to comment on it, not as a northerner nor as a southerner, as an anthropologist or sociologist, but as a Christian. It is to speak the truth about the brotherhood of man because one knows the Fatherhood of God. Not to speak this truth is to deny the nature of God. The truth spoken by the Christian is always the truth spoken in love and humility, but it must be spoken.

Some unidentified wit has described the kind of preacher not to become:

I humbly feel that my success, my power of attraction
　Is mainly due to following out this golden rule of action,

See all from all men's point of view; use others' eyes to see
    with;
And never preach what anyone could ever disagree with.

There is a common phrase that has within it an unchanging
kernel of truth; the preacher is called "to comfort the afflicted
and to afflict the comfortable." There is embedded in the heart
of the Gospel a discipline. Christians are called to take up their
cross and follow Christ. Part of discipleship is learning that "the
way of the Cross *is* the way of life" and that when a man loses
his life for Christ's sake he finds it.

It is the responsibility of the preacher to call his people to
lives of noble, disciplined service. It is for their sakes that he
preaches the strengthening Word of God. They cannot be
strengthened if they are deprived of the greatness of that Word.

A preacher who is known by his people as one who is their
pastor will be understood when he is a prophet. They will listen
to him preach in church if he is involved in their lives at home.
A preacher who is known as one who himself lives under the
total dimension of the Gospel, and who is precise and accurate
in presenting the facts of any social situation, will discover that
his people will stand by him and support him in his preaching
of the living Word of God.

3. The Minister as Priest

The life of the priest is sacramental, not because he is a
priest, but because he is a Christian. The Christian has a sacramental life because he has been baptized into the Body of Christ,
and Christ thereafter lives in him. Sacramentally he is the
"bearer of Christ" wherever he goes.

The office of the minister, however, is sacramental because it
is given him by the church for the purpose of preaching the
Word of God and administering the sacraments. This ministry,

as we have seen, is part of the total ministry of Christ, which is the ministry of the church, that is, of the people who are baptized into the Body of Christ.

Certain members of that Body are commissioned by ordination to carry out specific functions of the total ministry of the church; in popular usage these are the "ministers." The church gives them the authority of the office by the power of the Holy Spirit. Or, to put it another way, the Holy Spirit gives them authority through the church to exercise their ministry. That authority has to do with preaching the Word and administering the sacraments.

A commonly accepted meaning of the word "sacrament" is that it is "an outward and visible sign of an inward and spiritual grace given unto us; ordained by Christ himself, as a means whereby we receive this grace and a pledge to assure us thereof." [10]

The sacramental principle affirms the importance of all material things and goods. It says that a handclasp, a kiss, sex are good—as they are used sacramentally in life. It is this high regard for the material elements in life that caused William Temple to say that Christianity is the most materialistic of all religions. It is not a disembodied "spiritual" religion, but is concerned with the very stuff of life. Since Christ took upon himself our flesh by entering as fully as he could into the total experience of what it means to be a man, we can enter fully into all human life. All life may be outward and visible signs of inward and spiritual grace.

Within the church this sacramental principle focuses on Baptism and Holy Communion. Dr. Dora Chaplin has given this description of what the sacramental principle in the church means: "The sacramental life is the life in which the individual accepts the offering of God's own Self through God-chosen means. Through the simple acts of washing and feeding, made

[10] *Book of Common Prayer,* p. 292.

holy in Baptism and in the Eucharist, a Christian discovers his unique relationship with God as a member of the Body of Christ. A life opened up to God and transformed by him is called the sacramental life." [11]

This theme can be stated very simply. Christians know themselves to be members of a family, the head of which is Jesus Christ. They have been brought into that family through Baptism. Baptism is the action of the Holy Spirit, carried out by the ministry in behalf of the whole church. Whatever the human relationships were that caused a person to be baptized—parents who "made the arrangements" or friends who "influenced them" —Christian people recognize that it was the Spirit of God working through those relationships that was ultimately responsible. It was that Spirit that took the initiative to call them into the family of Christ and to declare through Baptism that they are in fact children of God, members of Christ, and inheritors of the Kingdom of Heaven.

The "outward and visible sign" is water administered in the name of the Father, and of the Son, and of the Holy Ghost. This act is performed by the minister who is carrying out this particular sacramental function of the whole church.

It is this same principle that is at work when the minister acts as priest in the service of the Lord's Supper or Holy Communion. There again the priest is at one with the people in the offering made and he is at one with Christ in his absolving the people. He is man-in-the-middle. The minister in his office combines the function of administering the sacrament and pronouncing absolution in the name of God.

The act of worship is not done by the minister acting alone, but by the total ministry of the church. In that act the minister by virtue of his office (not his person) stands in behalf of the people before God and in the name of God before the people.

[11] Dora Chaplin, "Preparing for the Sacramental Life" in *Living Thankfully*, H. R. Landon, ed. (Seabury, 1961), pp. 33–34.

In the total corporate action the "outward and visible sign" of bread and wine becomes by the action of the Holy Spirit "the Body and Blood of Christ, which are spiritually taken and received by the faithful in the Lord's Supper." [12]

The office of the priest, then, has the dual nature of administering the sacraments and pronouncing absolution in the name of God. It is this combination at the very heart of the sacramental principle of Christian life that underlines the central meaning of the office of the priest. Frederick Denison Maurice put it this way:

> According to the idea which has always existed in the Christian Church, the same person to whom the function of absolving is committed has also the function of administering the Eucharist. These two duties never have been separated, and it is most needful that they should be contemplated in their relation to each other; for if the Eucharist be that act in which the worshipper is especially brought into direct communion with his Lord, that act in which the mere human and visible agent is most entirely lost and forgotten, or only contemplated as one who bears witness that he whom he serves is a living and actual person, we must suppose that this is a key to the whole character of the office, in whatever way it may be exercised.[13]

The life of the minister is sacramental, not because he is a priest, but because he is a Christian; his work is sacramental, not because he is a good Christian, but because he is carrying on the work of the minister as priest.

4. The Minister as a Teacher

Any man teaches by his life. A minister is no exception. He is a teacher, first of all, simply because of what he is as a person.

---

[12] *Book of Common Prayer*, p. 293.
[13] F. D. Maurice, *The Kingdom of Christ* (SCM 1958), Volume II, pp. 131–132.

How he speaks, how he acts, what he reveals of himself—all have bearing upon how well he teaches the Christian faith.

He also teaches, however, in the specific exercise of his ministry. He teaches when he is a pastor, when he preaches, and when he is a priest. His teaching gifts are closely bound up with his personal gifts and are expressed through all sides of his entire ministry.

Simply in the course of the normal pastoral care of his people he has limitless opportunities to teach: a couple comes for marriage instruction, and learns what a Christian marriage is; a child is to be baptized, and both parents and Godparents are taught the meaning of baptism and their responsibilities; in times of personal crises—sickness, family difficulties, financial reverses, frustrations, disappointments, and failures—the meaning of fidelity can be taught and ways opened to discern God's hand in the midst of the crisis; when death comes, grief and bereavement can be placed within a Christian framework, so that all the natural impulses may be expressed and fulfilled finally in relation to God.

The minister is also a teacher when he preaches. He is called upon to express the truth of Almighty God as he has experienced that truth in his own life and as it has come through the experience of generations of Christian men and women. It is not only his personal knowledge that he is called upon to give, but the knowledge of the church. As he brings to bear upon the human situation the insights that are revealed through the Bible, he will be constantly explaining, teaching, describing the mighty acts of God, particularly as they culminate in the life, death, resurrection, and ascension of Jesus Christ.

And it is as a priest also that he teaches. "Actions speak louder than words." As a priest he is acting; he does things; he breaks bread; he passes the cup; he baptizes; he absolves. It is in the drama of the liturgy that the priest acts out the meaning of the Christian faith. Those actions have a power to teach.

Although the minister will teach as a pastor, as he preaches and as he is a priest, he will also carry on the teaching function of the ministry directly because he is a teacher. The qualities that a minister needs in order to teach effectively are the same that any teacher needs. In his book *The Art of Teaching,* Gilbert Highet lists them very directly.[14] A good teacher, he says, must (1) know his subject, (2) like it, and (3) like his pupils.

1. So far as the church is concerned, the people have a right to expect that a minister will know what he is talking about. Luther says that a preacher "must know his stuff and keep at it." [15] This does not mean that the minister must be a specialist, but he should have a competent grasp of his subject. He should "know his stuff."

2. To say that a minister must like his subject is simply to say that he must be drawn to and excited by the central affirmations of the Christian faith. He must enjoy dealing with the issues of religion and be persuaded of the truth of the Christian faith. When he presents the case for Christianity, he will do it with enthusiasm.

3. Finally, to like the pupils is to say once again that the minister is to express loving concern for all his people, adults as well as young people. This means that he will like them and be drawn to them simply because they are people. If he likes them as people—and not simply because they are objects to be taught —he will find that they have a ready ear to listen.

Although ministers will have varied opportunities for teaching, depending upon the particular circumstances of their church, in general most ministers will be able to teach in at least the following ways.

In the first place ministers are responsible for the Christian education program. This is carried out most often through the teaching of the church school, although there is today an added emphasis upon the teaching of adults. In some churches with

[14] G. Highet, *The Art of Teaching* (Vintage), pp. 12–33.
[15] E. A. Luther (Erlangen ed.), 59, 194; quoted in H. R. Niebuhr *et al. op. cit.,* p. 134.

sufficient resources a professional religious educator may be responsible for the church school program, although the teaching itself generally is carried on by volunteers. The atmosphere in which the teaching is carried on will be established, however, by the minister himself. If the minister is wise he will always maintain some teaching relationship with young people. This personal firsthand contact will enable him to keep in touch with the spirit of the younger generation and to know the questions they are asking. They will refresh his spirit with their vigor and candor. And they will keep him humble.

Second, it is almost always possible for a minister to give one or more series of lectures during the course of a year. To place himself under the regular discipline of periodically presenting a series of talks will keep him on the growing edge of his own studies and year after year will build an increasingly secure foundation for his people's understanding of the Christian faith. Indeed, there will be many people in the community who will come to hear a lecture who will not come to church. Lectures, therefore, may be bridges over which particularly the intellectuals in a community who are not members of any church may be touched.

In the formation of study groups, the minister is not so much a lecturer as he is a leader. At times it is even better for him simply to be a member of the group. They may take an infinite variety of forms and subjects: Bible study, social issues, "great books," prayer, personal religion, vocation, and many others. Small groups made up of men and women in particular professions may meet best under auspices of the church to discuss their distinctive witness as Christians.

Finally, one of the responsibilities of the minister as teacher is to teach his people how to pray, for without prayer they will not appropriate for themselves and for their lives the truth of the Christian faith. It is one of the areas in the Christian life where people need help—not so much to urge them to pray, because the pressures of life will see that they do that, as to help them to pray intelligently and "through Jesus Christ our Lord."

The teacher of prayer must himself be a man of prayer. He should give orderly, clear, concise instructions in how to pray. He should be specific and to the point. He should always give his people freedom from himself so that they may be taught by God. Prayer must be done by the person himself if there is to be growth. This means directly in relationship to God. The minister here, as in the preaching office, has the primary task of relating his people to God. He should not stand in the middle any longer than to introduce them to each other. Then he should step aside so the relationship may be developed freely in accordance with the individual's need and his own response to the leading of God. The key for this kind of spiritual counsel is: support as long as necessary, and then freedom. The ultimate teacher is God, and the teacher must set his pupils free from himself so that they may know God personally.

5. The Minister as Administrator

If you were to ask the average parish minister to evaluate the importance of his different roles in order, he would list them as follows:

> Preacher
> Pastor
> Priest
> Teacher
> Organizer
> Administrator

When you ask the same minister, however, to put in order their roles in accordance with the time actually spent in the ministry, the order would be this:

Administrator
Pastor
Preacher-Priest
Organizer
Teacher

During the average workday of the minister, he spends two-fifths of his time in administration.[16]

It is perfectly obvious that administration is here to stay. It is essential, therefore, that the minister have a clear idea of the purpose of administration in order that he may not only learn to accept it as one of the facts of life but also do it intelligently and creatively.

Ministers are called both to shepherd a flock and to administer an institution. How that institution is administered will determine in some measure how well the flock is shepherded. It will also determine in part how the church carries out its mission.

Administration has to do with the incorporation of the pastoral, preaching, priestly, and teaching functions of the ministry within the local congregation so that their ministry in the world may be strengthened. As the minister himself incorporates the different functions of the ministry into one, so does the total ministry of the church incorporate all aspects into one. It is finally one ministry of the entire church. Administration is part of that ministry, and the minister himself is charged with responsibility for it.

In general all administrative matters may be divided into two categories: (a) things and (b) people.

a. To talk of things is to talk about budgets, bills, buildings, boilers, and basements. Things represent the material aspects of life; they are terribly important, and they may be used for good or for ill. It is the purpose of the administration within the

[16] Samuel Blizzard, Report, Russell Sage Foundation, *Christian Century*, April 25, 1956.

church to see that these are all used for building, for strength, and for good.

Stewardship, for example, means a responsible accounting of money. Except under unusual circumstances a budget is meant to be balanced. There should be a responsible stewardship of money spent to balance the sacrificial giving expected of the people. In almost every instance the attitude of the minister toward these "incarnational matters" will determine the attitude of the people. If he takes pride in taking care of the property where God has placed him to minister so that there may be an attractive quality about it for those who pass by, his people will quickly share that pride. If he is conscientious himself about teaching and practicing stewardship, his people will follow his lead.

There is nothing romantic about boilers, and yet boilers are very important if a building is to be heated. Within the total framework of a Christian theology that rests upon the Incarnation where Christ hallows all the material aspects of life, oil for the boiler is as important as stained glass in the windows. As the minister remembers that he is called to serve man where he is, he will put as much effort into budgets as into preaching, for both have to do with the strengthening of the local segment of the body of Christ for the work of the church in that place. Administration is God's work no less than the rest of a minister's work.

b. One of the popular platitudes of the day is, "Things are to be used and people are to be loved." This, like most platitudes, happens to be true.

The point is that people are more important than budgets. Budgets are to be used so that people may learn how to love one another. People are not to be used in order that budgets may be raised.

Therefore the minister will look upon every administrative task as an opportunity to relate people to one another so that in their deepest concern for one another the body of the church may be strengthened. He will determine whether administration is to be used for people or whether people are to be used to strengthen the administration.

Committees are always made up of people. No matter what the task, it will be carried out by people. The principle that applies here: shared responsibility, common respect, and the truth to be spoken in love that the task may be done. The greater the participation of lay people, the greater the strength. In recent years the ruling bodies of congregations have increasingly been brought together on the basis of functional responsibility. That is to say, the chairmen of committees charged with various responsibilities in the administrative tasks of the church meet together and out of their diverse interests there is built a common *esprit de corps* as responsibilities and concerns are shared.

The minister who is an effective administrator will discover that lay people will help him carry out his pastoral responsibilities. Members of the Body of Christ are meant to minister to one another. It is not the sole responsibility of the pastor; indeed, his pastoral function is a shared one. It is in part out of his pastoral concern that he will create within the parish small groups that will be able to help him carry out the pastoral function of the total ministry of the church.

A wife, for example, whose husband had left her was introduced by the minister, after three sessions of personal counseling, to a group of four women. Those women had not lost their husbands, but each had suffered a personal tragedy. They were able to accept the new woman with sympathy, to stand beside her so that she knew that she was not alone, and in time to give her sufficient strength to go back into life with courage. This was a "redemptive fellowship" in the best sense of the word.

From one point of view it can be said that this is the purpose of administration: that the people may minister to one another.

They are called to tasks in order that all in the church may in their love for one another recognize that the Lord is God; it is he alone who is to be served; they are his and not their own. So is the mission of the church carried out.

A Reminder

Before concluding this chapter, it may be well to remind ourselves that although the minister is a many-sided man, as we have seen, he is above all a *man*. He is a person who fills an office. Therefore, what he *is* is related to what he does, and what he does is sometimes not nearly so important as what he is. This is simply to say of the ministry—it takes a man.

Enough has been put before you now to see that these many sides that make up the ministry are important, taxing, and challenging. The carrying out of the various functions are what the minister does. How he does them determines the quality of the ministry where he is, and what in turn in large measure determines the quality of the ministry of the laity where he is. In the long run the quality of the minister, more than any other single factor, determines the quality of the church in that place.

The minister does not need great natural gifts. He can be a not very effective speaker; he need not be overly bright; he may have limited personal abilities. He does, however, have to be a man.

What this means can be stated very briefly.

1. A Christian minister is *involved* with his people. He is a part of them, part of their life, part of their sin, part of their glory. When one of them dies, he dies a little bit. When one of them is victorious in a struggle, he lifts his head a little higher. He is engaged. He is right in the middle of his people.

2. A Christian minister is not called to be successful; he is

called only to be *faithful*. Success in the ministry is often evaluated on the basis of the number of people in one's congregation, the number of new members admitted each year, the size of the budget. These criteria have nothing to do with the minister's actual success. That is determined by one factor only: his fidelity to his task. Nobody knows what that is except the minister himself and God.

A minister is not trying to win a popularity contest. He is trying to be an ambassador of Christ. He does not, therefore, have to consider himself someone who is at the beck and call of people simply to gratify their own wishes. He is at the beck and call of God alone. He is called to serve God, and to serve his people in his name. He is accountable, therefore, only to God—and his only task is to be faithful to him.

3. A Christian minister is a man of *prayer*. All that has been said of the place and importance of prayer for his people is equally true for himself. It is in the long inner watches of his soul with God that he works over his experiences in the light of his learning, offers them to God, and asks the Holy Spirit to make them and him acceptable to God for his service. This is interior; it is quiet; it is hidden; it is where he as a man really lives.

It is this that provides the source of inner strength and of resiliency (of inner toughness almost) that he needs as a man in the face of the task he is called upon to perform. It is this that keeps him, the man-in-the-middle, from breaking. Grace within his soul brings the strength for the day, for God gives this always equal to the task.

4. A Christian minister is a man who knows *whose he is*. He is God's man. Therefore he does not have to waste time and energy pretending he is somebody else's man—either his own or his church's or his people's. He is responsible to God alone, and he knows that God is above all else faithful.

A young boy once asked his minister if he were God. After

being assured that he was not, he then asked: "But you are a friend of God, aren't you?" The quality of a minister's life must make it clear to little children, as to adults, that he is indeed a friend of God.

Because his trust, as his ministry, is in God, he carries out the many sides of the ministry, showing to his people and to the world, as he is able, the fruit of God's Spirit in him—

Love
  Joy
    Peace
      Longsuffering
      Gentleness
      Goodness
      Faith
      Meekness
      Temperance.[17]

In time—in God's time—this man who is God's minister becomes the new man that all God's people become in this world or in the life to come. Together with his people in the sharing of their common life here and in the breaking of bread they have a foretaste of that life that will be shared fully with one another and with him who will be their host at the Heavenly Banquet.

[17] Galatians 6:22–23.

8

Varieties of Ministries

ALTHOUGH THERE IS BUT ONE MINISTRY, WHICH IS CHRIST'S, it is exercised in a variety of ways. Indeed, it can be said that it is exercised in as many different ways as there are Christian individuals, both lay and clerical. The purpose of this chapter is to consider some of the specific ways by which this ministry is carried out and to look at some of the practical matters that are involved.

1. The Parish Ministry

The "gathered community" in the local congregation is the basic cell in the body of the church. The ministry to this congregation is the most common ministry, and it is here where the day-by-day life of the church is carried on and its mission made real.

Historically in most of America the parish church was the single church of a village or of a limited geographic area, but by the end of the eighteenth century this parochial boundary system was outgrown, so that today there may be not only many local congregations in one neighborhood, but several of them may even belong to one denomination. The congregations originally reflected the makeup of the community because the members lived there. This is still the case in the suburbs, rural areas, and small towns, but in many of the urban areas the members have moved away, although many have retained membership in their city churches. As we have seen in Chapter IV, this raises for the local church the serious problems of both "absentee membership" and failure to relate to the community. These are of critical importance to the minister of the urban church.

The parish minister is concerned with strengthening the life of the congregation for its mission. In his preaching and conduct of services on Sunday, as by his pastoral care throughout the week, he strives to serve his people that they may serve the community where they live and work. He is himself related to the life of the community, but his greatest influence comes normally through his involvement with his people in their homes, in their work, in all the common associations of their lives, and preeminently in their corporate worship of God.

2. The Teaching Ministry

The field of education provides a wide opportunity for a variety of ministries. The religious educator is primarily concerned with carrying on a teaching ministry through the local church. Such a person is responsible for the normal church school program for children and young people, and for a continuing program of education for adults. There are also opportunities for specialists in religious education on the administrative staffs of various denominations and occasionally of interdenominational bodies.

Openings for teachers exist on every level of American education. On the secondary-school level, particularly in independent schools, ministers are given the responsibility of teaching courses in religion or sacred studies. In some schools particular efforts are made to engage clergy who are qualified to teach in fields other than religion. Frequently, teaching positions in schools are combined with chaplaincies where a man assumes the responsibility for the formal conduct of religious exercises and to stimulate the formation of groups concerned with moral and ethical values, both for discussion and for action.

On the level of higher education there has been, since the Second World War, a steady increase in the number of positions made available in the field of religion. Departments of religion now exist in an increasing number of colleges and universities. One of the most effective arms of the church is in strong departments of religion where matters of faith are subjected to the same rigorous scrutiny as all other disciplines. In a community dedicated to education, one of the most stimulating challenges is to be responsible for the presentation of religious history and thought. Although most of the teaching in colleges is with undergraduates, there are in some of the great universities of America opportunities for teaching on the graduate level as well.

Finally the possibility of teaching in a seminary must be mentioned. The seminary teacher is usually not only a scholar and a teacher, as are all professors in graduate school; he is also a churchman. This means that he has some responsibility not only to his discipline and to his students but also to the church at large. Insofar as the seminaries are genuine "centers of learning" for the church, he is in a particularly significant position to make a very real contribution.

3. The Ministry of Chaplains

Reference has already been made to *chaplains* who serve on the faculty *of secondary schools*. These are either church schools that belong formally to some denomination, or independent schools where the work is carried on within a broad religious framework. Even in most of the former, however, the character of the work is intended to serve the interest and needs of young people of a variety of church backgrounds.

The chaplain normally is given the responsibility for the conduct of the chapel services in accordance with the traditions of the school. He serves as the adviser to student groups who are concerned particularly with the moral and ethical issues found in the school itself and in placing them within some religious dimension. These groups may be responsible for the Campus Chest, or in stimulating interest in the missionary enterprise, or in assisting people, particularly students, in the undeveloped areas of the world.

Frequently the chaplain finds himself the spokesman for a religious perspective in general, and will discover that much of his ministry is in relationship to fellow faculty members. As he comes to be accepted as a colleague who presents his religious concern and material with integrity, honesty, and openmindedness, he discovers that he is accepted on those terms by his colleagues and that he can carry on an important ministry to teachers and administrators as well as to students.

The role of *chaplain on the college and university campus* is much the same but within a much more complex community of learning. Although he will himself belong to one denomination, his ministry as chaplain of the institution will be carried out generally on an interdenominational basis. He will be faced with the challenge of associating on as deep a level as possible with the widest variety of human beings and at the same time remaining committed to his Christian convictions. A man who has an interest in the life of the intellect, who enjoys relating himself to young men and women, many of whom will examine, but only a minority accept, his position, will find that this ministry is one of the most stimulating and creative on the American scene.

As with the school chaplain, his ministry will also in part be with the faculty. Again, as he is discovered by the faculty to be open to points of view other than his own, honest in the presentation of the Christian position, and clearly concerned about people simply because they are people, he will in time come to minister to faculty and faculty families. His ability to preach intelligently and persuasively will be of utmost importance. In some instances it will be possible for him to provide opportunities for interested members of the faculty to discuss religious issues and the relation of their particular disciplines to them. These groups may become one of the most satisfying aspects of his ministry and an effective arm of the church on the campus.

Most of the denominations have *denominational chaplaincies* in larger college and university centers. There the chaplain who represents a particular denomination has substantially the same opportunities and challenges as the college or university chaplain except that his ministry is more typically associated with those who belong to his communion. He conducts services and leads discussion groups within a particular denominational framework. The broad-gauge chaplain who is eager to help in every way the work of the church of Christ, and therefore identifies himself with other denominational chaplains in carrying on a more complete ministry, makes an invaluable witness to the cause of the church.

Chaplaincy to the Armed Forces is another type of ministry that is of critical importance in time of war, and in time of peace of great significance to the men in the Armed Forces and to their families. It is one of the broadest areas of service that enables a man to identify himself with his generation and with his country's cause under God. It is a ministry that is able to touch young men who for the first time in their lives, in most instances, are away from home; and in certain stations it is a ministry to families not unlike the normal ministry in a local congregation. As in other kinds of chaplaincies, responsibility is given for the conduct of services of worship, for pastoral counseling, and for guidance in discussion and study groups. Usually there are certain collateral duties that are assigned chaplains in the Armed Forces. These usually represent an opportunity for the chaplain to be put in touch with men through relationships other than religious, and they provide helpful bridges into the lives of the men and their families. In somewhat the same way and for the same purposes chaplaincies are provided in hospitals under the Veterans Administration.

Hospital chaplains are increasingly being recognized as important in the healing of the whole man. The hospital chaplain —whether in the general hospital or the mental hospital—is being thought of more and more as one of a team, all the members of which are concerned with the healing ministry. The chaplain takes his place alongside the doctor, the nurse, the social worker, the psychiatrist. Hospital chaplaincies are particularly rewarding for men who are concerned about personal counseling in depth and who wish to carry on a ministry in conjunction with a psychiatrist. Clinical training, which is now recognized as a part of theological education in many seminaries, is usually conducted under the supervision of hospital chaplains who are qualified as supervisors.

Chaplaincies in prisons, reformatories, and other institutions for those who are unable to live creatively in society also offer opportunities in the ministry. Institutions such as foster homes, homes for disturbed children, homes for the aged, and nursing homes established to meet particular social needs will, under certain circumstances, make provision for chaplaincy services.[1]

4. The Modern Missionary

The ministry of the missionary overseas is essentially the same as that of the ministry everywhere: to bring to people an under-

[1] Additional information on institutional chaplaincies may be obtained from the Department of Pastoral Services, Commission on Ministry in Institutions, 475 Riverside Drive, New York 27, N.Y.

standing of themselves as children of God and brothers of one another. There are of course significant sociological and cultural forces in the mission field that affect the form in which the Gospel is presented, but there is no change in the heart of the Christian faith or in the declaration of God's mind toward all men. The external "packaging" is always adapted to local circumstances, but the content is the same for every age and for every culture.

Thus the ministry of the missionary may be carried on in certain areas primarily by teachers and doctors; in others it may be by evangelists and priests. Sometimes the Word will be preached in words; at other times it will be spoken entirely by deeds. There will be in some instances a ministry carried on in forthright and unmistakable Christian terms; in other instances it may be exclusively in the form of service projects, and concerned only with meeting the physical needs of people.

The modern missionary is under particular obligation in two areas. He must understand the language, society, and religion of the people he has come to serve, and with the latter he must identify himself as fully as possible. No longer is it possible to go among other people and live in isolation from them in foreign compounds. This means invariably an intensive period of language study before going overseas and some education in depth concerning their history, culture, and social mores.

Furthermore, the missionary is required to have a very clear understanding of the relation of the Christian religion to the religion of the people where he is to minister. When he speaks of Christians as the "chosen people," it is essential that his hearers understand precisely the way in which this Biblical phrase is used: "chosen" for the sake of other people so that they may know the true God. He will not present Christianity as standing over against other faiths, but as the fulfillment of them. Since he knows that God has "left not himself without witness" [2] he

[2] Acts 14:17.

will search for those evidences of God in the religion of his people to establish as many points of contact with them as possible. Then he may speak of the Christian religion as that which completes all other religions. In the process he will not confuse Western folkways with the Christian faith and insist on conformity in nonessentials, such as the type of clothing to be worn.

Perhaps the spirit of this contemporary missionary enterprise is best illustrated by the story of an elderly devout Buddhist who one day, hearing the story of Jesus Christ, said, "Yes. This is the God I have been searching for all my life." To such a one the Gospel comes as Good News to complete both his search for God and what he has already known of God.

The missionary from the West will not only identify himself with the people he has come to serve; today he will also identify himself with the church that already exists in foreign lands, and in many instances will carry on his work under the direction of the nationals of the country. These younger churches in Asia and Africa have now raised up second- and third-generation Christians, and the leadership of the Christian enterprise there quite properly has passed largely into their hands. Domination by the older churches is nearly a thing of the past, and when this process has been completed then the missionary movement will have come of age, for then all Christians will in fact know themselves to be members one of another, with deference paid to no group simply on the grounds of national origin.

5. Ministry in Religious Communities

The years since the Second World War have seen an increasing number of men and women turning to the specialized ministry of the religious life. The monastic movement has a heritage that goes back to the earliest years of the Christian era and bears witness to a fundamental side of the Christian life: the work of prayer. There are in every era some men and women who by virtue of their particular aptitude and vocation are called to serve both God and man in this special way. Those called to this work of prayer and worship undertake to live in a community bound together by the three vows of obedience, chastity, and poverty. Both clergy and laymen participate in this ordered community life.

These communities vary greatly in their makeup and purpose —some are separated from the world to devote themselves exclusively to prayer; some are concerned to carry on works of service in the world; and others are a mixture—but all hold to a common life of prayer as central to their existence. In the Protestant Episcopal Church, for example, a great variety is found among the eight communities for men and fourteen for women. In the Reformed Church in France a striking contribution to church unity has been made by the community at Taizé.

Adaptations of the traditional religious communities have been made in some places. The Iona Community in Scotland, for example, under the leadership of George McLeod, has recaptured the spirit of this old Celtic monastery, and has become one of the established centers for retreats and for renewal for laymen as well as for clergy. Parishfield in Michigan has in a similar way given expression to the same spirit and search for renewal in the modern world.

6. Team Ministries in Urban Areas

As the character of the inner city changes and former residents go to the suburbs, the churches have been faced with the task of finding new ways to minister to the people who have come in in large numbers. Many of the new arrivals are unchurched; they do not speak English; they are among the lowest-paid group of unskilled laborers; they have lost touch with old familiar landmarks. There has been a general breakdown of the traditional family structure, and a high rate of juvenile delinquency is normal.

One of the most promising of the new forms of ministry has been the team ministry developed in some of the urban centers of America. The key has been the corporate nature of the ministry, where all share in a common ministry, though with special responsibilities; and with this has been the identification of the ministers with the people they serve. The churches are for the most part unpretentious storefront churches; the ministers and their families live in the area; and they maintain an "open-door policy" so that anyone in need may always find some temporary refuge.

The team may include not only clergy but also social workers, group recreation leaders, teachers, and lawyers. It represents an attempt to have the total needs of the community met by the total ministry of the church, and is always expressed in terms of social action and community concern, as well as in the more traditional forms of church life. The outstanding pioneer in this field has been the East Harlem Protestant Parish in New York City,[3] founded after the Second World War by a group of young ministers concerned to deal directly and realistically with the needs of the people. It is interdenominational in nature, and has established a pattern that is being duplicated in other urban areas.

7. The Ministry to Industry

In order that the church may have some ongoing relationship to industry and to the people involved in its world, industrial chaplaincies have been developed in recent years. The form that

[3] East Harlem Protestant Parish, 2050 Second Avenue, New York 29, N.Y.

this has usually followed has been an extension of the pastoral ministry through a chaplaincy service provided for the people within a particular industry or company. The chaplain himself may be engaged by management and labor together, or by a particular denomination or by a local council of churches. It is a ministry that focuses its attention upon personal and family problems and incorporates the services provided by social agencies in the community as well as by the churches.

Another type of ministry, also concerned about industry, which is still in its pioneering stages and which promises to be one of the most creative ministries of the contemporary church is represented by the Detroit Industrial Mission.[4] The approach here is not directed to the concerns of the pastoral ministry but rather to the study of the basic structure of an industrial society, its impact upon the lives of the people who belong to it, and what its relation, if any, is to the Christian Church. This ministry at the present time is, therefore, occupied primarily with learning, study, and research. Rather than giving answers, the minister asks questions. He is involved as much (and sometimes more) with industrial life as with church life. Some of the ministers, for example, work as skilled laborers in factories. They are concerned to find out how participation on the part of the modern industrial man (whether of ownership, management, or labor) in the life of the church has any bearing upon his working life. This type of approach and inquiry holds promise for the development of other, similar ministries in the future.

8. Miscellaneous Ministries

The field of *communication* offers opportunities for exercising unusually creative ministries for those with special aptitude

---

[4] Detroit Industrial Mission, 24699 Grand River Avenue, Detroit 19, Mich.

and training. In a day when communication is increasingly audiovisual, ministries may be carried on in radio and television broadcasting and programming. Religious journalism, particularly in the magazine field, is also an influential field for those who can write arrestingly and intelligently.

The whole area of *administration* within the organizational structure of the churches provides another important avenue for the ministry. The varied work of the church in its many divisions and concerns requires the supervision of an able and dedicated staff. Opportunities for ministering in this way are provided by such organizations as local and state councils of churches, the National Council of Churches of Christ in America, and the World Council of Churches.

Beyond the structure of the organized church there are many institutions that are motivated by a religious spirit, that are concerned to be of service to men, and that, while not officially a part of the church, do serve as an arm of the church. Examples are the Young Men's Christian Association, the Young Women's Christian Association, and other social, family, and welfare organizations.

All these positions that have been described as "Miscellaneous Ministries" can of course be filled as well by laymen as by clergymen.[5] The work of the ministry does not invariably require the services of an ordained minister. It is important for us to have in mind that there is a specific ministry of the laity, and it is that that we shall now consider.

[5] The most useful single article describing church vocations is *Laborers Into His Harvest*. It may be obtained for 40¢ from the *International Journal of Religious Education,* P.O. Box 238, New York 10, N.Y.   J. O. Nelson lists forty-eight different kinds of positions, many of which are open to laymen, in his *Listing of Church Vocations*. This includes a helpful bibliography of guidance materials and may be obtained from the National Coucil of the Churches of Christ in the U.S.A., 475 Riverside Drive, New York 27, N.Y. Specific questions may be directed to the Department of the Ministry of your own church. The best person to ask for guidance first of all is your pastor.

The Ministry of the Layman

The layman has a ministry as well as the clergyman. As a member of the Body of Christ he shares in the total ministry of the church. The layman exercises his ministry in a different way from that of the clergyman, but it is as essential a part of Christ's ministry.

The ministry of the layman is carried out in the world. It is the exercise of a man's gift in that way that he believes best enables him to serve both God and man. He may do it as a teacher, a banker, a clerk, a laborer, "a butcher, baker, or candlestick maker." The key to the ministry of the layman is the same as that of the clergyman: to do what he is doing for the service of God and man. It is to realize that his gifts are not his own, but God's, and that they are to be exercised to his glory in expressing love of him and of man.

For a man to have a deep conviction that God has work for him to do in the normal exercise of his natural gifts is to have an understanding of his ministry as a layman. A man's decision not to enter the ordained ministry of the church may be just as clearly a decision in response to the will of God for him as another's is to enter that ministry. In either case the considerations have to do with how the individual can best take his part in exercising the wholeness of Christ's ministry.

Dietrich Bonhoeffer in his book *Prisoner for God* puts it this way:

The Christian must plunge himself into the life of the godless world without attempting to gloss over its ungodliness with a veneer of religion, or trying to transfigure it. He must live a "worldly" life and so participate in the suffering God. He *may* live a worldly life as one emanicapted from all false religions and obligations. To be a Christian does not mean to be religious in a particular way, to cultivate some particular form of asceticism (as a sinner, a penitent, or a saint) but to be a man. It is not some religious act that makes a Christian what he is, but participation in the suffering of God in the light of the world.[6]

"To be a Christian . . . [means] to be a man." Once a man has come to the conclusion that his ministry can best be carried out as a layman, he should then go about his work and do it as intelligently and as well as he can. He is meant "to be a man." He should, therefore, be just that: a husband, a father, a teacher, a painter, or whatever. He should be content to be that which he is. This is to be a Christian.

The ministry of the layman, then, is carried on as he goes about his business to live with (to use a phrase of Jacques Ellul) a Christian "style of life." Christians living with this style make it clear by the way in which they live that they are able to sit loosely to the things of this world. They know that their work, their possessions, their success are not ends in themselves, and that they do not have to agonize about them. They know that they are not their own. They are the Lord's. If they live they are the Lord's; if they die they are the Lord's. As they go about their business of living they are trying to do it to express their love of him and of their fellowmen. On this level there is no difference between their ministry and that of the ordained clergyman.

Variety in a Day

A minister's day is what he makes it. There are no time clocks to regulate his working hours; he has no immediate superior to direct his activities; there is no authority to whom he must report his accomplishments. He is free to do nothing all day; he is free to respond to the normal demands as they occur; he is free

[6] *Prisoner for God* (The Macmillan Company, 1959), p. 166.

to select those pressures to which he will give way and those he will ignore. In the long run what he makes of his day will determine what he makes of his ministry.

Given the almost infinite variety of ministries, as well as the variety of personalities, it is impossible to describe with any degree of accuracy a typical day in the life of a minister. Studies have been made, however, of how the clergy spend their time, and the daily activities of 480 rural and urban ministers have been classified. The survey was made of the actual breakdown of the ministers' time, concentrating upon his "professional work day," and not including his personal and family activities. Here are the results:

> The professional work day of the cooperating ministers averaged a few minutes less than ten hours. Rural men reported a work day of nine hours and 17 minutes. That of the urban minister was ten hours and 32 minutes. Considering all ministerial informants, almost two-fifths of their total work day was spent as administrator. Slightly more than one-fourth was devoted to the pastor role. Preaching and priestly activities took up almost one-fifth of the work day. Organizing consumed more than one-tenth of the work day. The residual time (about one-twentieth) was devoted to teaching. This order of priority from most time to least time (administrator, pastor, preacher and priest, organizer, teacher) was the same for both urban and rural parish ministers.
>
> An incidental but revealing item of intelligence is the time parish ministers devote to sermon preparation and to stenographic work each day. The average time devoted to sermon preparation is 34 minutes for rural men, 38 minutes for urban clergyman. The time taken up by stenographic tasks is one hour and four minutes for both country and city men.[7]

The comment is sometimes made, "I cannot understand what a minister does except on Sundays." This survey provides a partial answer. To be sure, on Sunday the minister functions

[7] Samuel Blizzard, Report, Russell Sage Foundation, *Christian Century*, April 25, 1956, p. 509.

primarily as preacher, priest, and teacher. What he is able to do on that day, however, is determined in very large measure by how he has spent the other days of the week. If it is time well spent, the few people who are touched day by day will recognize it. The real fruit of his weekday work, however, will be seen as it is reflected in his ministering on the Lord's day when he feeds his flock who are gathered to hear the Word and to worship God.

A Word about Money

A graduate of a seminary can count on a beginning salary that will range between $3,000 and $6,000, depending upon his family circumstances. Salaries for the parish ministry are usually between $8,000 and $12,000, although some may go as high as $15,000 and above. In addition, housing, or a housing allowance, is almost without exception provided. Sometimes utilities are included as well, to cover the cost of heat, light, and telephone. An increasing number of congregations are providing an automobile allowance, which may be anywhere between $300 and $800 annually. Finally, some retirement provision or pension plan is underwritten in whole or in part by the local church or denomination. The share paid for the minister may range from 5 percent of his salary (with the man making a similar contribution) to 15 percent paid entirely by the church.

It goes without saying that no man who is interested primarily in financial return will enter the ministry. At the same time he can expect that those whom he serves faithfully will reward him accordingly. It is clear that the churches are increasingly responsible about their financial obligations to their pastor. The minister whose primary concern is to carry out his ministry to the best of his ability will find that as a by-product reasonable financial security is given. As he seeks first God's Kingdom and his righteousness, all these things are added unto him.

This is not to say, however, that there are no problems in the ministry in the contemporary church. There are. And it is to these that we now turn.

9

Some Crosses, and Hints on Bearing Them

IN THE MINISTRY, AS IN EVERY CALLING, THERE ARE PROBLEMS. A Christian minister is not exempt either from the professional burdens that come to him because of his ministry or from the human difficulties that beset him simply because he is a man. Some of the problems are "built-in" in the sense that they are part of the structure of the contemporary ministry. Others are the personal problems that arise from a minister's own life and individual situation.

In either case they may be considered as crosses that may be borne for the sake of God and therefore provide the best means for a truly effective ministry. We shall consider four such crosses.

1. The Tension Between the Minister's Image of His Work and that Held by the Laity.

The minister tends to consider his role in one way and his lay people to consider it in another way. There is not a commonly accepted image of the office and work of a minister today, and the result is confusion, conflict, and tension.

In the study previously referred to conducted by Dr. Samuel W. Blizzard, 1,111 clergymen educated in both college and seminary cooperated in presenting their picture of this conflict.[1] This survey makes it perfectly clear that the clergy have one set of priorities in mind for the accomplishment of their tasks and that their people have another. Ministers tend to think of themselves primarily as preachers, priests, teachers, and pastors. Yet in the day-by-day work of the ministry top priority is taken by their role of administrators. They feel best qualified to fulfill the role of preacher, teacher, and priest, and least able as organizer and administrator. The sum of the matter is this:

> No matter how different ministers' ideas of what is important in the minister, all wind up doing substantially the same thing. It is perfectly apparent how largely the social roles of Protestant parish ministers are conditioned and defined by the requests of parishioners, the denominational program and the culture of the community. It is not nearly so clear at the parish level, however, how much a minister's religious ideology or normative orientation has to do with what he actually does as a minister. Furthermore, there appear to be basic ambiguities in the church structure itself. The minister is urged to spend much time organizing and administering programs. The national church body is at the same time failing to give him an adequate theological understanding of these offices. That is the minister's dilemma.[2]

In other words, the minister cannot always do what he wants to do, feels qualified to do, and enjoys doing. He is under pres-

[1] This research project was conducted under the auspices of Union Theological Seminary in New York and the Russell Sage Foundation. Four other seminaries participated in the project: the Protestant Episcopal Seminary, Alexandria, Va.; the Louisville Presbyterian Seminary, Louisville, Ky.; the School of Religion (Disciples), Butler University, Indianapolis, Ind.; Garrett Biblical Institute, Evanston, Ill. Through the Department of Town and Country Church and the Department of Urban Church, National Council of Churches, twenty-two Protestant denominations cooperated.

[2] Samuel Blizzard, Report, Russell Sage Foundation, *Christian Century*, April 25, 1956, p. 509.

sure to respond to the needs of his church as an organization, to do what his parishioners want, and what the denominational authorities apparently want. The pressures of the culture and the organizational church seem to put emphasis upon success evaluated by numbers and by statistics.

Criteria for the *effective* minister were considered by the ministers themselves to be ranked in the following order: character, an outgoing personality, and skill as a pastor-counselor. Criteria for the *successful* practice of the ministry were, however, considered in the following order: general ability in performing the practitioner role, cooperation in denominational programs, and an outgoing personality. Dr. Blizzard's comment is, "The dominant criteria appear to have secular, rather than theological over-tones." [3]

This type of conflict is seen in a number of ways. The minister is eager, for example, to find time for study in order that he may be an effective priest, pastor, and teacher; yet in the urban ministry the average minister gives, on the average, only twenty-seven minutes a day to general intellectual activity. He recognizes the need to develop a specialized ministry if he is to be effective, and yet he considers himself to be no more than "a general practitioner." He feels a primary responsibility to the members of his local congregation, and yet he is called upon to minister also to people who belong neither to his congregation nor to any other and to serve in some capacity in organizations in the community at large. In brief he stands within a welter of stresses, conflicts, and tensions. [4]

[3] Blizzard, "The Parish Minister's Self-Image of His Master Role," *Pastoral Psychology,* December, 1958, p. 32.

[4] See "Role Conflicts of the Urban Protestant Minister," in *The City Church,* Vol. VII, No. 4, Sept., 1956, pp. 13–15. Other articles that deal with this conflict and reflect the findings of this survey are as follows: "Parish Minister Bench Marks for Theological Education" (much of this material is contained in an article published in the *Union Seminary Quarterly Review,* Vol. XI, No. 2, January, 1956, pp. 45–50, entitled "The Training of the Parish Minister"); "The Protestant Parish Minister's

One clergyman in a suburban church on the West Coast found himself in the middle of such a conflict as it centered upon the issue of the Christmas bazaar. He felt that in his role as pastor of that church he had no particular responsibility for sale of goods at the bazaar, even though the profit was used to support the budget of the church. On the other hand the ladies of the women's organization felt that because they put so much time into working for the bazaar the least that the minister could do would be to support it with his presence. Some of them said, "We're doing this for you." His reply was that he couldn't care less about the bazaar; that he was concerned about the set of values that caused moneymaking in that church to be the most important enterprise in the life of the people; and that he could not in good conscience support it. Some of the ladies felt that if this was his feeling there was no reason why they should support the church at all. When he absented himself from the two-day bazaar one year, three women resigned from the parish.

Around such matters as these are feelings hurt, parishes occasionally divided, and ministers sometimes broken. In themselves they are almost always minor issues. They simply reflect the basic confusion and conflict in the differing images that the ministers and the people have of the office and work of the minister.

Two simple steps are called for in learning how to live with this particular cross. First of all it is important to recognize the simple fact of life that there is this conflict of images. There is no point in denying it, rebelling against it, or giving up to it. To deny it is to be either dishonest or unintelligent; to rebel is to be immature; and to give in is to capitulate prematurely.

The second step is to distinguish between what can be

Integrating Roles," *Religious Education,* Vol. LIII, No. 4, July–August, 1958, pp. 374–380; "The Parish Minister's Self-Image of His Master Role," *Pastoral Psychology,* Vol. 9, No. 89, December, 1958, pp. 25–32.

changed and what cannot be changed in the structure. It is more important to maintain a pastoral relationship with people than it is to win minor victories over minor matters. Church bazaars on the whole are very silly things to divide parishes. So long as the pastoral relationship remains strong, most issues can be resolved by intelligent and patient consideration.

This matter of being able to distinguish the more important from the less important is a crucial key. Reinhold Niebuhr has put it in the form of a prayer: "Give me the serenity to accept what cannot be changed; give me the courage to change what must be changed and the wisdom to distinguish one from the other."

2. The Tension Between a Minister's Responsibility to His Work and to His Family

The clergyman rose from the supper table just before the dessert was brought in by his oldest daughter. "I'm sorry," he said, "but I have to leave to get down to the committee meeting at the church by 7:15." As he walked to the door, leaving his wife and four children at the supper table, she called to him, "You know, John, we're waiting for the time when you show as much love to us as you do to your people." As he drove out of the driveway he said to himself, "I'll make it up to them somehow." But in the bottom of his heart he was afraid that he never would.

How can a minister be a good minister to his people and still be a good husband to his wife and father to his children? This is the problem. It lies closer to the heart of his personal life than any other. No minister is free of this cross unless he has remained unmarried.

A minister who has responsibilities to his work and to his family finds that there is always some tension between the two and that in certain crises it can explode. This conflict of loyalties is not, of course, limited to clergymen, for every man who has responsibilities outside the home faces the same problem. A doctor, for example, no less than a minister, is forced to decide either for his home or his office every day of his professional life.

There are, however, several distinctive difficulties that arise in ministers' families. One of them is cultural. There is no general understanding in our society of what a minister is and what his role is meant to be. This is particularly difficult for the minister's wife, because she is not certain what a minister's wife is supposed to be and do. Her three college friends, let us say, have married, respectively, a doctor, a lawyer, and a chauffeur. Everybody in our culture knows what doctors, lawyers, and chauffeurs are meant to be, and their wives take their own places accordingly. Not so with the minister's wife, however. Is she an assistant minister? Can she have friends of her own outside the church? Can she smoke? Suppose she doesn't believe everything her husband believes or what the church teaches? Can she have a life of her own?

The difficulties carry over into the home itself. Clergy families sometimes feel that they live in goldfish bowls where they are under the scrutiny of the church and community alike. Although this is not nearly so common now as it was a generation ago, it is still not unheard of for parishioners to walk unannounced into the parsonage because the house "belongs to us." Inasmuch as the local church board is not only technically the landlord of the minister but also his employer, it makes it awkward for him in negotiating such items as fresh paint, new wallpaper, and modern plumbing for the parsonage.

This leaves some kind of an impression upon children. Although in the long run children of the parsonage do no worse (and perhaps a little better) than do other children, the kind of life their father leads—and, more important, the kind of life people expect them to lead—does make its influence felt. Fiction (if not fact) testifies to what it means to be a P.K.—a preacher's kid. Rebellion is undertaken as the most effective way to establish independence and integrity of their own; and they become the Peck's Bad Boys who always smoke cornsilk behind the barn.

In addition, clergy and their wives are not exempt from the normal human difficulties that beset marriage and family life. They, too, have difficult in-law situations to deal with; they may have to cope, as many others do, with sexual problems and adjustments; they also have to wrestle with financial pressures and struggle to balance budgets. These down-to-earth human issues provide the raw material out of which marriages are made. This is as true for clergy marriages as for others. The recognition of this fact is the place to begin.

The marriage of a clergyman is the same as the marriage of any Christian person. It is a man and a woman who are in love, not a priest and a woman. The man may be a priest, but if the woman loves his priesthood rather than his manhood it will be an unbalanced marriage.

If a minister and his wife—like any couple—in their meeting and knowing one another always understand that they are meeting and knowing God—that it is he with whom they are dealing —then the fundamental structure of their response to God is made possible. So long as their response to their problems is the response of a Christian man and a Christian woman bound together in holy matrimony, then their problems can be dealt with creatively, for God as well as they will be dealing with them.

The fundamental difficulty for a minister's marriage is the difficulty of apparent divided loyalty. The key word is *apparent*.

The principle is this. If God is responsible for the human love that a minister knows in his relationship to his wife, and if God is also responsible for that man being called into the ministry, then it is the same God calling a man to be a whole person. The response of the minister is meant to be a total response of the whole person to the one God who is the giver of every gift. Within these terms there can be no such thing as divided loyalty. There is one loyalty—that loyalty is to God. It is expressed in the loyalties to his wife and to his work. If all life is from God, it is meant to be all of a piece, even though it appears at times to be divided and fragmented.

The answer in part rests with the minister's wife. She has it when she is content to be simply herself. She finds herself married to a man who happens to be a minister. She accepts this as part of who he is, and she goes about her life as a person who is in love with him and naturally wants to help him as much as she can. She neither rebels against his work, if she does not share his faith; nor does she usurp his position because she does share it. Her best help is simply to be herself—a woman in love with a man—and not be overly anxious about any role she thinks she is supposed to fill as the minister's wife.

The key is to be natural. A visitor to a church was once impressed by the number of people who commented to him about what a lovely wife the minister had. The phrase that he heard time and time again was, "She is perfectly natural." As a result she had won a place in the affection of the people. When he mentioned this to her at the end of his visit, she replied: "That is very easy to explain. In our first parish I tried so hard to be a 'good minister's wife' that I never was myself. As a result I was a miserable failure. When we came here, however, I discovered I was pregnant. Each year now for the past three years I've had a baby. I haven't been able to be anything other than myself simply because I have not had the time. So when they say that the good thing about me is that I'm perfectly natural, they're just as right as they can be. It has been a great lesson to learn."

The primary concern of the minister's wife, then, will be to help her husband be the best minister he can be—just as any wife would want to do all she can to make her husband the best he can be in his chosen profession.

Once a minister's wife understands that her primary responsibility is to be herself—a wife who loves her husband—then two further words can be said. First, she will want to take her place in the life of the congregation on the basis of her time, ability, and interest. She should feel under no coercion to take special positions of leadership because she is the minister's wife.

The other word is that she should not confuse her husband with God—or his word with God's Word. Here the answer to the problem will be largely in his hands. He will be tempted to assume that because he can exercise authority in the name of God in his general ministry he can do the same in his own home. There the authority is not his, but it is God's and it rests upon the common acceptance by both of them of what God's will is. It cannot, in the minister's home, anymore than in any other home, be interpreted and mediated only by one member. The minister in relation to his wife is "but a man." Marriage rests upon a common life under God with a common understanding and a common response.

Christian marriage for the minister, no less than for the layman, depends upon both man and wife remaining open to one another and to God. When this is done, then the issues that arise can be squarely faced. Some issues will be solved. Other issues will not be solved, but must be lived with.

These issues may become crosses. When issues arise for a minister and his wife that they cannot morally avoid, then they become crosses to be shared together. It should come as no surprise that there will be crosses in the ministry, nor should it be surprising that this apparent conflict of loyalties between family and work is one of them.

Yet it is the crosses they bear together that bind them closest to each other. It is *not* having their own way that enables them to carry on an effective ministry. It is indeed just this fact that makes it possible for the cross to become a means of grace and of strength. In the family life of a Christian minister it is this that binds a man and a woman together on the deepest level of their existence.

The minister and his wife, therefore, regardless of the tensions within any particular situation, are always given an opportunity to respond to them as a potential means of grace from God. Then they can deal with them creatively. The cross brings them closer to each other and together closer to God who having given them their cross then helps them bear it.

3. *"A Prophet Is Not Without Honor . . ."*

In a town in the Southwest the minister had been dropped from the school board. The motion for his removal came after he had preached a sermon urging the members of his congregation to support "the law of the land" and to begin to make provision for the integration of the public school system. Outwardly everything went on as before. The board of deacons did not ask for his resignation, but contributions dwindled. No one attacked him publicly, but he was asked by no civic organization to make any speeches. His wife was not ostracized, but conversation with her friends was limited more and more to superficial topics of the weather and parties. She commented: "I haven't had a real conversation with a real person in this town for over a year. They are perfectly polite, but there is no question about how they regard my husband and me. I wish we could get a job somewhere else." Her husband commented, "But, my dear, we have a job."

A minister must be prepared to face the conflict between saying what his people want to hear and what he believes God wants them to hear. He finds himself torn between wanting to please them and wanting to please God; between being loyal to an institution and to the Head of that institution, Christ; between respecting the convictions of his people and his own inner convictions. This is the problem referred to earlier about the role of the minister to "comfort the afflicted and afflict the comfortable." It has to do with the minister as prophet and the constraint he stands under to preach the Word of God in such fashion that he can say, "Thus saith the Lord," so that his people will know it.

He can do this as he bears certain fundamental precepts in mind.

1. He has a responsibility to know the facts. When he talks about social issues and the implications of the Gospel for the life of men where they live and work, he has a primary responsibility to be accurate, precise, and honest.

2. He has a responsibility to take into consideration the honest disagreements that may be held by members of his congregation. A minister is free to give voice to his conscientious principles only after he has taken into serious consideration the equally conscientious scruples of those who oppose him, and particularly of those to whom he has been called to minister.

3. He has the responsibility to distinguish between positions and people. One minister has commented, "I must be certain when I speak *against* a point of view that everybody understands that I am speaking against their *positions* and not against them." This is to affirm the fundamental importance of the pastoral relationship in the life of a congregation. If the minister is known as one who loves his people and cares for them, he will be listened to when he speaks the truth. If they know that a minister has at heart what is, in his judgment, good for them under God, they will listen. People do not expect to be coddled by a minister; nor do they have any respect for him if he fawns on them. Christian people know that there is judgment involved in the Gospel, and they will respect a man when that judgment

is expressed—as long as they know it arises out of his love for them and for their common God.

In other words, the best way to be heard as a prophet is to be a good pastor.

4. He has the responsibility, finally, to do the right as God gives him to see the right. The moral principle here is a clear one: when you are uncertain about what God wants you to do, keep silent. When you know what he wants you to do, act.

It is no easy task for an ordinary Christian minister to act like a Christian statesman. Yet this is precisely what he is called to do. He is meant to bring a Christian perspective into all the dark recesses of human life, and yet he cannot avoid being in the battle himself. It is a cross, to be sure, but the cross can be a banner for the Christian life. Carrying it is the best way that he can minister effectively to his people.

4. The Problem of Oneself

"The only real problem I have is myself." This comment describes the situation of everyone who recognizes that what he is as a person determines how he responds to the demands of life. The three kinds of pressures that have been described above represent problems that exist within the ministry today. They are there regardless of the personality of the minister. Whether they are borne well or ill will depend in large measure upon the man himself. It is for this reason that he can say, "The only real problem I have is myself."

The help he needs with this problem is provided by the Christian faith. Beginning with his honest acceptance of himself as he is, he can be set free from any overpreoccupation with himself, with his sins, with his weaknesses, and failures. He can be set free from taking himself too seriously or even taking his sins too seriously.

Another way of saying this is to recognize that all Christians have been set free by Christ—and this includes ministers. They do not have to be justified by their good works; they do not have to establish themselves in the eyes of God or men by their success as ministers; they are not called on to make it clear to the world how able they are. They do not have to prove their ministry or themselves by the effectiveness of their preaching, pastoral care, administration—or anything else under the sun.

If the Christian Gospel means anything, it means simply this: we are justified by God. We do not have to justify ourselves. We are free from the little tyrannies of success, power, prestige, and all the rest by Christ. Indeed, best of all, we have been set free even from ourselves.

Therefore all we have to do is get on with the job.

This does not mean, of course, that we are to pay no attention to what we are as persons. It does mean that our confidence and our hope is in God, and not in ourselves or anything that we do.

The inevitable blows of life will make a minister—just as they will any human being—either bitter and cynical or gentle and therefore strong. There is a strength that comes from being broken and humbled. When a minister can embrace all life, including its trials and tribulations and his own brokenness, then his ministry cannot fail to be enriched and deepened.

One minister was asked how he found the strength to go on after his wife died. "Well," he said, "I wasn't certain what I was going to do. It seemed to me that the bottom had dropped out of everything. So I went away for two days to try to find out why this should have happened. I didn't then find any answer to that question, but I did know what I was meant to do: to come back and go about my job as a minister. Since then to the best of my ability I have tried to do this because I think it is perfectly clear that this is what God wants me to do. I am beginning to suspect that the reason this happened to me has to do with what God intends me to do with my life as a minister. There is beginning to be a rightness about the whole experience. I don't have the whole picture yet, but God does. In the meantime I am trying to get on with the job that he has given me to do." That man filled his ministry.

At times when people are going through deep waters the greatest help that ministers can give them is to make it clear, not so much by what they say as by what they are, that life is saying to them: "Go out into those deep waters. Go just as far as you can. Put your feet down; the ground there is firm. It will hold you. Try it and see." He will speak with authority if he has stood on that bottom himself.

Things are not as they appear to be, says the Christian. Part of the ministry is to help people see that God always works under the surface in a hidden fashion. Indeed, it is in the worst experiences of life that God comes to give his greatest strength to people. If the minister knows this on the basis of his own experience his ministry will have no end of usefulness.

The sum of the matter, therefore, is this: Christian people are never surprised to have crosses to bear. Ministers are never surprised to find that they have certain crosses to bear in their ministry. They are no heavier burdens than Christian people bear in all walks of life.

The "professional" crosses that come within the structure of the contemporary ministry can always be borne if the last "personal" cross of the self can be borne. That is a man's heaviest cross. Ministers, as all Christian people, have a framework for life provided by their Christian faith that enables them to show forth, just as all Christians are called to show forth, not only with their lips but also in their lives, the power that God gives—especially through their crosses—and thus to know the peace and the joy the world can neither give nor take away.

10

The Heart of the Matter:
How Do You Decide?

THE PRINCIPLE POINT TO BE MADE IN THIS CHAPTER IS THAT
the decision to go into the ministry must be your own. The
essential question is: Do you want to? If you do—and are
qualified—go.

There are, of course, other considerations that must be taken
into account, and we shall examine them. They all, however,
are important only because they will enable you to make up
your mind intelligently about what it is that you want to do.

To put this negatively for the sake of emphasis: Do not go
into the ministry because (a) the church needs ministers, (b)
your parents, or anyone else, want you to, or (c) you think you
ought to. All these factors again may have some bearing upon
your decision, but they are secondary. The primary consideration is your own free, mature choice to serve God and man.

You will come to that choice because of the experiences of
your life, through which you may believe God is calling you to
the ministry. You then are free to respond. Make your response
your own.

I

Your Aptitude

The first step is to have as objective a picture of your ability as possible. Begin by getting the wisest counsel you can about your own nature, gifts, and abilities.

The composite picture will probably come from three sources. The first is the picture that appears on the record as a result of educational and psychological testing. There is a wide range of psychological and psychiatric examinations that determine a man's native ability for different vocations. There are vocational counselors who can be of assistance.

Some of the tests that have been found to be useful are the following: Rorschach, Thematic Apperception Test, Szondi (for experimental purposes), American Council of Education Psychological Examination, Cooperative Botany Test: Part II, Interpretation of Experiments, Evaluation Modality Test, Strong Vocational Interest Test for Men, and Allport-Vernon-Lindzey Study of Values.[1]

It is probably not necessary to add that these should be administered by a professionally trained psychologist and accompanied by an interview in order that the whole personality may be evaluated. The tests do not in themselves predict that a man will be a success or failure in the ministry, but they are extremely helpful in coming to understand and characterize an individual.

The second source for help in filling out the picture of yourself will come from friends and mature counselors. Can you

[1] These tests are used by Van Waters Associates, Personnel Consultants, Boston, in their screening of applicants for the ministry. H. S. Sullivan, *The Psychiatric Interview* (Norton, 1954), especially "The Personified Self," is also recommended.

get from them any idea of what kind of person you are? How do you appear to them? Are you tight, tense, withdrawn, introspective, unable to relate to others? Or are you an open, relaxed individual with an outgoing personality? Do people look upon you as one who is interested in them? Do they open up to you naturally?

What do older friends who are in the ministry think of you as a possible candidate for the ministry? Have you been encouraged by any of them? Has your pastor ever spoken to you about the ministry? Do you think they are interested in encouraging you for your sake, or because they want another recruit for the ministry? How do your professors judge your ability?

The third source for the total picture will be that provided by yourself. What is your own picture of yourself? What are your strong points? What are your weak ones? What can you do well? What do you like doing? What bores you? What can't you do at all? What do you have your heart set on in life? Are you willing to be used by people, or do you prefer most of the time to use them? When you think of the ministry, do you think of it as a means for you to attain fulfillment, or do you think that your fulfillment will be attained because you have been useful to people?

Go back and read those questions on pages 46 and 47 of Chapter 3. Do you answer them affirmatively on the whole?

Analyze the Needs of Contemporary Society

Analyze them on two levels: the social needs of mankind for justice, order, and equality; and the personal needs of people for acceptance, forgiveness, and love.

1. Make a list in order of priority of what you believe society (mankind) needs most: Greater scientific knowledge to unloose further the creative forces in nature? A strengthened international order to put those creative forces to work for the good of all mankind? A heightened moral and ethical sense of values?

With regard to the underdeveloped nations of the world, what do they need: Nuclear power, industrialization, democracy, social order, a system of ethical values? Or what?

2. On the level of personal needs what is it, in your judgment, that individual people need most: Nourishment and medical care for their bodies that they may be healthy? Learning, that they may know how to use the minds that they have been given? To be accepted, so that they have a sense of belonging? To be forgiven? To be loved? To have some religious faith so that they may answer those human questions of where they come from and are going to? To have resources given them so that they may journey through life with power? To have some sense that life lived on the most intimate personal level is related somehow to the most ultimate meaning in existence possible?

Put the Two Together

On the basis of your own religious faith at this moment, to what extent do you believe that God is involved in any relationship between yourself, as analyzed under your aptitudes, and society as analyzed under the needs of the world?

To what extent do you believe that God is related to your own sense of values and to the world in which you find yourself? As you try to find out what it is that makes you tick as a human being, do you think that God is involved? Do you think that

that is the same God who has any relationship to the world of nations and peoples? Do you think that there is any connection between the type of life you live and the life that the peoples of the world are living?

As you look back over your own life, can you see ways by which you believe God has led you, or at least been involved in your life? Do you think you could say as you look back that you see a possibility that maybe he has brought you to this place for the purpose now of making your life count most for the world and for the people in the world?

If your answer to the last question is "yes" or "yes, perhaps," then you are ready to take the second step.

II

The second step is: "Sit on it."

This is a time for silence. With the possible exception of one or two intimate friends, this is not the time for speaking to people. If you have now the idea that you might one day go into the ministry, let that idea remain in the back of your mind for some time. Do not act upon it immediately. Do not try to force an answer. Live with the question. Keep it to yourself. It may become more pressing, or it may go away. The great danger here is that you will come to a premature decision— either for it or against it. Offer the question and the concern to God, and leave it to him for the time being.

A Reminder About Motivation

You will, at this juncture, be concerned to examine your own motives. You will wonder whether you are thinking of going into the ministry to run away from something; whether you look upon the church simply as a refuge; whether you are afraid of life. You will ask yourself whether you could earn a living elsewhere; or whether you are thinking of the ministry primarily out of weakness.

The word here is: Don't worry about mixed motivation. It always will be mixed. It always will be very complicated. It will be very difficult for you to be absolutely clear about the basic motivation that prompts you to take any action in life. This kind of clarification comes only in retrospect.

What appears to be the motivation a man has at the moment frequently turns out with the passage of the years to be not the motivation at all. How hard it is to look into the heart of anyone else—equaled only by the difficulty of looking into one's own inner heart.

If the question of your going into the ministry persists after this period of looking within, then go to three or four people who know you well and whom you trust and ask them what they think. Ask your wife, a close friend, a trusted older counselor, a clergyman. If the general tenor of their reply is "Yes, I can see you in the ministry," then you will have to take it more seriously. If the answer is negative, "No, I can't possibly see you in the ministry," you will have to wait some more to see if the question persists.

In time you must come to a tentative decision. It is a decision that no one can make except yourself. It will be one of two answers. The first, "No, as I look back I cannot see how God has been involved in bringing me to this place for the purpose of going into the ministry, and in any case I cannot see myself in the ministry." The alternative answer is, "Yes, I think I can see where God has brought me to this place, and as I look ahead I can see myself in the ministry."

If the answer is "yes," then there are two further tests to be made.

III

1. The Test of Circumstances

By this is simply meant: are the circumstances of your life such that it is practical for you to consider the ministry?

Do you, for example, have sufficient *educational background* to enter seminary for theological education? Do you have a college degree? If not, is it possible for you to get one? If you do not have a college degree, you will be able to enter a seminary only under unusual circumstances.

One young man has had it in his mind to enter the ministry for twelve years. He has, however, only an eighth-grade education. During those twelve years, he has worked in a factory. He has been unable to take sufficient night courses to complete even a high-school education. These circumstances being what they are, he has in effect failed to pass this test, and he will not enter the ministry.

Or, to take another illustration, how are your *financial circumstances?* Are you already under such a burden of debt that you could not responsibly discharge that burden and still go to seminary? Is there any likelihood that you could change these circumstances in the next years?

One young man, who is well qualified educationally, made the decision to enter the ministry. He had, however, a debt of five thousand dollars. He went to work, and over a period of three years repaid that debt. He then was free, so far as his financial responsibilities were concerned, to enter the ministry.

Are your *family circumstances* such that you can enter the ministry? If you are married, does your wife approve? If she disapproves of your decision can you be a responsible husband

and still carry it out? (The answer is "no.") If you have children, can you responsibly uproot them from their present schooling and environment, and perhaps jeopardize their education so that you can go into the ministry?

It is obvious that there is a close relationship between financial circumstance and family circumstance. A single man can act as a free agent in a way that a married man never can. A married man has made his own previous free choices and therefore commitments to responsibilities. He is not free to repudiate his family, or to disregard what is right for them.

On the other hand, young men who are single may find that repudiation of a family's position is required if they are to enter the ministry. One graduate student in physics made the decision to enter the ministry, and applied for admission to seminary. When his father heard of this, he wrote him: "If you persist in your decision to go to seminary I shall refuse to give you one red cent to place upon the altar of superstition and bigotry." In such a situation the son must then decide whether he is to make his own mature decision in life, even though this may mean a cutting of parental ties, or whether the ministry is not worth the cost.

Although that is an extreme example, it is not uncommon. One married man, an engineer with three children, decided at the age of thirty to go into the ministry. His father wrote him, "So long as you have made this decision, I never wish to hear from you again." The young man with the support of his wife carried through his decision.

It is difficult to evaluate precisely how much family support or the lack of it counts in a decision of this kind. Some men are nurtured in Christian homes where there is a natural acceptance of the ministry as an honorable profession, and a man may unconsciously be influenced to make an affirmative decision. On the other hand, there are many families where such a decision on the part of the son is a cause of disappointment, if not opposition. Yet some families with no religious background are proud when a son enters the ministry.

In any case circumstances will play a large part in helping you come to a decision. Your family, your education, your background, your money, all the circumstances of life will have some bearing upon your decision. If the circumstances are such that you can in a morally responsible and intelligent fashion continue with your plans to enter the ministry, then you have passed the circumstantial test, and can proceed to the next one.

2. The Test of the Church

Inasmuch as the ministry is Christ's ministry, and ordination is given within the church, its authorities also must be consulted. It is they who have the final decision.

The simplest way to proceed is to begin with your own minister. He will give you his own judgment and will advise you as to the next step to take. Generally speaking, you will be asked to appear before some group representing the local congregation. If they encourage you, you normally will be examined by the authorities of the church beyond the local organization— a church council, a group of presbyters, an executive secretary, a bishop, or some authority who can speak in the name of the church. That testing will usually consist of evaluating you as a person on the basis of your past record, and coming to some conclusion about your promise in the ministry. Normally there are educational, aptitude, and psychological tests to be taken, depending upon the requirement of the particular denomination.

If you pass the circumstantial test and the test of the church, there is then only one final question.

IV

The Final Test: Do You Want to
Enter the Ministry?

No one can answer this question except you. Do not try to put the question off on friends or on the church or on God. The question is not "Do you think you ought to go into the ministry? It is "Do you want to?" It must be a free, responsible decision of your own.

It can be put as bluntly as this, when you arrive at this point. The one who is asking you this question is God. He says, "John, what do you want to do?"

A minister was once counseling a group of men on the matter of Christian decision. He pointed out the necessity for any decision to be intelligent and morally responsible. Then he said to them: "If there seems to be no clear sign from God, what he is in fact saying is, 'What do you want to do?' And what he means is, 'What do *you* want to do?' He is a partner in your life, and he does not want an unwilling partner." So the real question is, What do you want to do?

One way to come to an answer is to make out some kind of timetable, so that a target date can be set when the issue will be resolved once for all.

Formulate as well as you can all the positive and negative factors. Go over the first four steps with care, evaluating your abilities, the needs of the world, the circumstances of your life, the position of the church. Weigh them in relationship to one another as intelligently as you can. It almost always is a help to do this by putting everything down on paper.

Then put the whole matter in the back of your mind; offer

it to God with a prayer that his will may be done by you; and think about it as little as possible.

Set a date, usually no longer than a month in advance, when you will come to a decision. On that day go to church. Offer your life and decision to God. Walk out of church. Do it.

If your decision has been "yes," God will hold out to you the blessing that he has for men who go into the ministry of the church.

If the answer is "no," God will hold out to you the equal blessing that he has for men who do not go into the ministry of the church.

Whatever you may do, plan to do it for the love of God— then do it.

God will bless you—in the ministry or out!

God bless you.

Amen.